VIEWS AND REVIEWS

ESSAYS

IN APPRECIATION

BY

W. E. HENLEY

Copyright © 2013 Read Books Ltd.
This book is copyright and may not be
reproduced or copied in any way without
the express permission of the publisher in writing

British Library Cataloguing-in-Publication Data
A catalogue record for this book is available from the
British Library

Contents

William Ernest Henley 1

Prefatory

A 'Frightful Minus'
His Method. 6
His Development. 8
His Results. 9
Ave Atque Vale. 11

Thackeray
His Worshippers. 12
His Critics. 14
Which Is Right?. 17
His Style. 18
His Mission. 20

Disraeli
His Novels. 23
A Contrast. 26
His Backgrounds. 27
His Men And Women. 28
His Style. 30
His Oratory. 31
His Speeches As Literature. 32
The Great Earl. 33

Alexandre Dumas

His Components. 35
Himself. 37
At Least. 40
His Monument. 43

George Meredith

His Qualities. 44
His Defects. 45
Another Way. 47
Rhoda Fleming. 49
The Tragic Comedians. 53
The Egoist. 53
In Metre. 55
The Fashion Of Art. 55

Byron

Byron And The World. 56
Byron And Wordsworth. 59

Hugo

His Critics. 63
Some Causes And Effects. 64
Environment. 66
Equipment And Achievement. 68
His Diary. 71
For And Against. 72
What Lives Of Him. 74

Heine
 The Villainy Translation. 80
 The Proof Of It. 81

Matthew Arnold
 His Verse. 84
 His Failure.. 85
 His Triumphs. 87
 His Prose. 90

Homer And Theocritus
 The Odyssey. 93
 The Idylls. 94
 Old Lamps And New. 97

Rabelais
 His Essence. 98
 His Secret. 99

Shakespeare
 A Parallel. 102

Sidney
 His Expression Of Life. 104
 His Fame. 105

Tourneur
 His Style. 106
 His Matter.. 107

Walton

    The Compleat Angler. 108
    Master Piscator. 109
Herrick
    His Muse.. 111
    His Moral. 113
    His Piety. 114
Locker
    His Qualities.. 115
    His Effect. 116
Banville
    His Nature. 117
    His Art. 118
Dobson
    Method And Effect.. 120
Berlioz
    The Critic. 123
    A Prototype.. 124
    His Theory Of Autobiography.. 126
George Eliot
    The Ideal. 129
    The REal. 129
    Appreciations. 130
Borrow
    His Vocation. 132

    Ideals And Achievements. 134
    Himself. 136

Balzac
    Under Which King? 137
    The Fact. 139

Labiche
    Teniers Or Daumier? 141
    Labiche. 143

Champfleury
    The Man. 146
    The Writer. 147

Longfellow
    Sea Poets. 149
    Longfellow. 150

Tennyson
    St. Agnes' Eve. 152
    Indian Summer. 153
    His Mastership. 155

Gordon Hake
    Aim And Equipment. 157

Landor
    Anti-Landor. 160
    His Drama. 161

Hood

    How Much Of Him? 163
    Death's Jest-Book. 164
    His Immortal Part. 167

Lever
    How He Lived. 169
    What He Was. 171
    How He Wrote. 172

Jefferies
    His Virtue. 175
    His Limitation. 176
    The General. 178
    Last Words. 179

Gay
    The Fabulist. 181
    The Moralist. 183
    After All.. 185

Essays And Essayists
    The Good Of Them. 186
    Generalities. 187
    In Particular.. 188

Boswell
    His Destiny. 191
    His Critic. 192
    Himself. 194

Congreve
- His Biographers And Critics. 198
- The Real Congreve. 198
- The Dramatist.. 200
- The Writer.. 202

Arabian Nights Entertainments
- Its Romance. 204
- Its Comedy. 206
- Sacer Vates.. 208

Richardson
- His Fortune.. 211
- Pamela.. 212
- Grandison. 214
- Clarissa. 215

Tolstoï
- The Man And The Artist. 218
- Ivan Iliitch. 220
- War And Peace. 221

Fielding
- Illusions. 223
- Facts. 225
- The Worst Of It. 226

William Ernest Henley

William Ernest Henley was born on 23rd August 1849, in Gloucester, England.

He attended Crypt Grammar School in Gloucester where the poet, scholar, and theologian, T. E. Brown, was headmaster. Brown had a made a huge impression on the young Henley and the two struck up a lifelong friendship. Henley claimed Brown to be "a man of Genius – the first I'd ever seen", and upon Brown's death in 1897, Henley wrote an admiring obituary to him in the *New Review*.

From the age of 12, Henley suffered from tuberculosis of the bone which eventually resulted in his left leg having to be amputated below the knee. According to Robert Louis Stevenson's letters, the character of Long John Silver was inspired by his friend Henley.

In 1867, Henley passed the Oxford Local Schools Examination and set off to London to establish himself as a journalist. Unfortunately, his career was frequently interrupted by long stays in hospital due to a diseased right foot which he refused to have amputated. During a three year stay at the Royal Infirmary of Edinburgh, Henley wrote and published his collection of poetry *In Hospital* (1875). This publication is noteworthy in particular for being some of the earliest examples of free verse written in England.

Henley married Hannah (Anna) Johnson Boyle on 22nd January 1878. The couple had one daughter together, Margaret, who died at the age of five and is reportedly the source of the name Wendy in J. M. Barrie's *Peter Pan*. Apparently she used to call Barrie her "fwendy wendy", resulting in the use of the name in the children's classic.

Henley's best-remembered work is his poem "Invictus", written in 1888. It is a passionate and defiant poem, reportedly written as a demonstration of resilience following the amputation of his leg. This poem was famously recited to fellow inmates at Robben Island prison by Nelson Mandela to spread the message of empowerment and self-mastery. He also wrote a notable work of literary criticisms, *Views and Reviews,* in 1890, in which he covered a wide range of works by prominent authors.

Henley died of tuberculosis in 1903 at the age of 53 at his home in Woking, and his ashes were interred in his daughter's grave in the churchyard at Cockayne Hatley in Bedfordshire, England.

PREFATORY

Suggested by one friend and selected and compiled by another, this volume is less a book than a mosaic of scraps and shreds recovered from the shot rubbish of some fourteen years of journalism. Thus, the notes on Longfellow, Balzac, Sidney, Tourneur, 'Arabian Nights Entertainments,' Borrow, George Eliot, and Mr. Frederick Locker are extracted from originals in 'London'—a print still remembered with affection by those concerned in it; those on Labiche, Champfleury, Richardson, Fielding, Byron, Gay, Congreve, Boswell, 'Essays and Essayists,' Jefferies, Hood, Matthew Arnold, Lever, Thackeray, Dickens, M. Théodore de Banville, Mr. Austin Dobson, and Mr. George Meredith from articles contributed to 'The Athenæum'; those on Dumas, Count Tolstoï's novels, and the verse of Dr. Hake from 'The Saturday Review'; those on Walton, Landor, and Heine from 'The Scots Observer,' 'The Academy,' and 'Vanity Fair' respectively; while the 'Disraeli' has been pieced together from 'London,' 'Vanity Fair,' and 'The Athenæum'; the 'Berlioz' from 'The Scots Observer' and 'The Saturday Review'; the 'Tennyson' from 'The Scots Observer' and 'The Magazine of Art'; the 'Homer and Theocritus' from 'Vanity Fair' and the defunct 'Teacher'; the 'Hugo' from 'The Athenæum,' 'The Magazine of Art,' and an unpublished fragment written for 'The Scottish Church.' In all cases permission to reprint is hereby gratefully acknowledged;

but the reprinted matter has been subjected to such a process of revision and reconstitution that much of it is practically new, while little or none remains as it was. I venture, then, to hope that the result, for all its scrappiness, will be found to have that unity which comes of method and an honest regard for letters.

W. E. H.

Edinr. 8th May 1890

A 'FRIGHTFUL MINUS'

Mr. Andrew Lang is delightfully severe on those who 'cannot read Dickens,' but in truth it is only by accident that he is not himself of that unhappy persuasion. For Dickens the humourist he has a most uncompromising enthusiasm; for Dickens the artist in drama and romance he has as little sympathy as the most practical. Of the prose of *David Copperfield* and *Our Mutual Friend*, the *Tale of Two Cities* and *The Mystery of Edwin Drood*, he disdains to speak. He is almost fierce (for him) in his denunciation of Little Nell and Paul Dombey; he protests that Monks and Ralph Nickleby are 'too steep,' as indeed they are. But of Bradley Headstone and Sydney Carton he says not a word; while of *Martin Chuzzlewit*—but here he shall speak for himself, the italics being a present to him. 'I have read in that book a score of times,' says he; 'I never see it but I revel in it—in Pecksniff and Mrs. Gamp and the Americans. *But what the plot is all about, what Jonas did, what Montague Tigg had to make in the matter, what all the pictures with plenty of shading illustrate, I have never been able to comprehend.*' This is almost as bad as the reflection (in a magazine) that Jonas Chuzzlewit is 'the most shadowy murderer in fiction.' Yet it is impossible to be angry. In his own way and within his own limits Mr. Lang is such a thoroughgoing admirer of Dickens that you are moved to compassion when you think of the much he loses by 'being constitutionally incapable' of perfect apprehension. 'How poor,' he cries, with generous enthusiasm, 'the world of fancy would be, "how dispeopled of her dreams," if, in some ruin of the social system, the books of Dickens were lost; and if The Dodger, and Charley Bates, and Mr. Crinkle and Miss Squeers and Sam Weller, and Mrs. Gamp, and Dick Swiveller were to perish, or to vanish with Menander's men and women! We cannot think of our world without them; and, children of dreams as they are, they seem more essential than great statesmen, artists, soldiers, who have actually worn flesh and blood, ribbons and orders, gowns and uniforms.' Nor is this all. He is almost prepared to welcome 'free education,' since 'every Englishman who can read, unless he be an Ass, is a reader the more' for Dickens. Does it not give one pause to reflect that the writer of this charming eulogy can only read the half of Dickens, and is half the ideal of his own denunciation.

His Method.

Dickens's imagination was diligent from the outset; with him conception was not less deliberate and careful than development; and so much he confesses when he describes himself as 'in the first stage of a new book, which consists in going round and round the idea, as you see a bird in his cage go about and about his sugar before he touches it.' 'I have no means,' he writes to a person wanting advice, 'of knowing whether you are patient in the pursuit of this art; but I am inclined to think that you are not, and that you do not discipline yourself enough. When one is impelled to write this or that, one has still to consider: "How much of this will tell for what I mean? How much of it is my own wild emotion and superfluous energy—how much remains that is truly belonging to this ideal character and these ideal circumstances?" It is in the laborious struggle to make this distinction, and in the determination to try for it, that the road to the correction of faults lies. [Perhaps I may remark, in support of the sincerity with which I write this, that I am an impatient and impulsive person myself, but that it has been for many years the constant effort of my life to practise at my desk what I preach to you.]' Such golden words could only have come from one enamoured of his art, and holding the utmost endeavour in its behalf of which his heart and mind were capable for a matter of simple duty. They are a proof that Dickens—in intention at least, and if in intention then surely, the fact of his genius being admitted, to some extent in fact as well—was an artist in the best sense of the term.

His Development.

In the beginning he often wrote exceeding ill, especially when he was doing his best to write seriously. He developed into an artist in words as he developed into an artist in the construction and the evolution of a story. But his development was his own work, and it is a fact that should redound eternally to his honour that he began in newspaper English, and by the production of an imitation of the *novela picaresca*—a string of adventures as broken and disconnected as the adventures of Lazarillo de Tormes or Peregrine Pickle, and went on to become an exemplar. A man self-made and self-taught, if he knew anything at all about the 'art for art' theory—which is doubtful—he may well have held it cheap enough. But he practised Millet's dogma—*Dans l'art il faut sa peau*—as resolutely as Millet himself, and that, too, under conditions that might have proved utterly demoralising had he been less robust and less sincere. He began as a serious novelist with Ralph Nickleby and Lord Frederick Verisopht; he went on to produce such masterpieces as Jonas Chuzzlewit and Doubledick, and Eugene Wrayburn and the immortal Mrs. Gamp, and Fagin and Sikes and Sydney Carton, and many another. The advance is one from positive weakness to positive strength, from ignorance to knowledge, from incapacity to mastery, from the manufacture of lay figures to the creation of human beings.

Views and Reviews

His Results.

His faults were many and grave. He wrote some nonsense; he sinned repeatedly against taste; he could be both noisy and vulgar; he was apt to be a caricaturist where he should have been a painter; he was often mawkish and often extravagant; and he was sometimes more inept than a great writer has ever been. But his work, whether bad or good, has in full measure the quality of sincerity. He meant what he did: and he meant it with his whole heart. He looked upon himself as representative and national—as indeed he was; he regarded his work as a universal possession; and he determined to do nothing that for lack of pains should prove unworthy of his function. If he sinned it was unadvisedly and unconsciously; if he failed it was because he knew no better. You feel that as you read. The freshness and fun of *Pickwick*—a comic middle-class epic, so to speak—seem mainly due to high spirits; and perhaps that immortal book should be described as a first improvisation by a young man of genius not yet sure of either expression or ambition and with only vague and momentary ideas about the duties and necessities of art. But from *Pickwick* onwards to *Edwin Drood* the effort after improvement is manifest. What are *Dombey* and *Dorrit* themselves but the failures of a great and serious artist? In truth the man's genius did but ripen with years and labour; he spent his life in developing from a popular writer into an artist. He extemporised *Pickwick*, it may be, but into *Copperfield* and *Chuzzlewit* and the *Tale of Two Cities* and *Our Mutual Friend* he put his whole might, working at them with a passion of determination not exceeded by Balzac himself. He had enchanted the public without an effort; he was the best-beloved of modern writers almost from the outset of his career. But he had in him at least as much of the French artist as of the middle-class Englishman; and if all his life he never ceased from self-education but went unswervingly in pursuit of culture, it was out of love for his art and because his conscience as an artist would not let him do otherwise. We have been told so often to train ourselves by studying the practice of workmen like Gautier and Hugo and imitating the virtues of work like *Hernani* and *Quatre-Vingt-Treize* and *l'Education Sentimentale*—we have heard so much of the æsthetic impeccability of Young France and the section of Young England that affects its qualities and reproduces its fashions—that it is hard to refrain from asking if, when all is said, we should not do well to look for models nearer home? if in place of such moulds of form as *Mademoiselle de Maupin* we might not take to considering stuff like *Rizpah* and *Our Mutual Friend*?

Ave atque Vale.

Yes, he had many and grave faults. But so had Sir Walter and the good Dumas; so, to be candid, had Shakespeare himself—Shakespeare the king of poets. To myself he is always the man of his unrivalled and enchanting letters—is always an incarnation of generous and abounding gaiety, a type of beneficent earnestness, a great expression of intellectual vigour and emotional vivacity. I love to remember that I came into the world contemporaneously with some of his bravest work, and to reflect that even as he was the inspiration of my boyhood so is he a delight of my middle age. I love to think that while English literature endures he will be remembered as one that loved his fellow-men, and did more to make them happy and amiable than any other writer of his time.

THACKERAY

His Worshippers.

It is odd to note how opinions differ as to the greatness of Thackeray and the value of his books. Some regard him as the greatest novelist of his age and country and as one of the greatest of any country and any age. These hold him to be not less sound a moralist than excellent as a writer, not less magnificently creative than usefully and delightfully cynical, not less powerful and complete a painter of manners than infallible as a social philosopher and incomparable as a lecturer on the human heart. They accept Amelia Sedley for a very woman; they believe in Colonel Newcome—'by *Don Quixote* out of *Little Nell*'—as in something venerable and heroic; they regard William Dobbin and 'Stunning' Warrington as finished and subtle portraitures; they think Becky Sharp an improvement upon Mme. Marneffe and Wenham better work than Rigby; they are in love with Laura Bell, and refuse to see either cruelty or caricature in their poet's presentment of Alcide de Mirobolant. Thackeray's fun, Thackeray's wisdom, Thackeray's knowledge of men and women, Thackeray's morality, Thackeray's view of life, 'his wit and humour, his pathos, and his umbrella,' are all articles of belief with them. Of Dickens they will not hear; Balzac they incline to despise; if they make any comparison between Thackeray and Fielding, or Thackeray and Richardson, or Thackeray and Sir Walter, or Thackeray and Disraeli, it is to the disadvantage of Disraeli and Scott and Richardson and Fielding. All these were well enough in their way and day; but they are not to be classed with Thackeray. It is said, no doubt, that Thackeray could neither make stories nor tell them; but he liked stories for all that, and by the hour could babble charmingly of *Ivanhoe* and the *Mousquetaires*. It is possible that he was afraid of passion, and had no manner of interest in crime. But then, how hard he bore upon snobs, and how vigorously he lashed the smaller vices and the meaner faults! It may be beyond dispute that he was seldom good at romance, and saw most things—art and nature included—rather prosaically and ill-naturedly, as he might see them who has been for many years a failure, and is naturally a little resentful of other men's successes; but then, how brilliant are his studies of club humanity and club manners! how thoroughly he understands the feelings of them that go down into the West in broughams! If he writes by preference for people with a thousand a year, is it not the duty of everybody with a particle of self-respect to have that income? Is it possible that any one who has it not can have either wit or sentiment, humour or understanding? Thackeray writes *of* gentlemen *for* gentlemen; therefore he is alone among artists; therefore he is 'the greatest novelist of his age.' That is the faith of the true believer: that the state of mind of him that reveres less wisely than thoroughly, and would rather be damned with Thackeray than saved with any one else.

His Critics.

The position of them that wear their rue with a difference, and do not agree that all literature is contained in *The Book of Snobs* and *Vanity Fair*, is more easily defended. They like and admire their Thackeray in many ways, but they think him rather a writer of genius who was innately and irredeemably a Philistine than a supreme artist or a great man. To them there is something artificial in the man and something insincere in the artist: something which makes it seem natural that his best work should smack of the literary *tour de force*, and that he should never have appeared to such advantage as when, in *Esmond* and in *Barry Lyndon*, he was writing up to a standard and upon a model not wholly of his own contrivance. They admit his claim to eminence as an adventurer in 'the discovery of the Ugly'; but they contend that even there he did his work more shrewishly and more pettily than he might; and in this connection they go so far as to reflect that a snob is not only 'one who meanly admires mean things,' as his own definition declares, but one who meanly detests mean things as well. They agree with

Views and Reviews

Walter Bagehot that to be perpetually haunted by the plush behind your chair is hardly a sign of lofty literary and moral genius; and they consider him narrow and vulgar in his view of humanity, limited in his outlook upon life, inclined to be envious, inclined to be tedious and pedantic, prone to repetitions, and apt in bidding for applause to appeal to the baser qualities of his readers and to catch their sympathy by making them feel themselves spitefully superior to their fellow-men. They look at his favourite heroines—at Laura and Ethel and Amelia; and they can but think him stupid who could ever have believed them interesting or admirable or attractive or true. They listen while he regrets it is impossible for him to attempt the picture of a man; and, with Barry Lyndon in their mind's eye and the knowledge that Casanova and Andrew Bowes suggested no more than that, they wonder if the impossibility was not a piece of luck for him. They hear him heaping contumely upon the murders and adulteries, the excesses in emotion, that pleased the men of 1830 as they had pleased the Elizabethans before them; and they see him turning with terror and loathing from these—which after all are effects of vigorous passion—to busy himself with the elaborate and careful narrative of how Barnes Newcome beat his wife, and Mrs. Mackenzie scolded Colonel Newcome to death, and old Twysden bragged and cringed himself into good society and an interest in the life and well-being of a little cad like Captain Woolcomb; and it is not amazing if they think his morality more dubious in some ways than the morality he is so firmly fixed to ridicule and to condemn. They reflect that he sees in Beatrix no more than the makings of a Bernstein; and they are puzzled, when they come to mark the contrast between the two portraitures and the difference between the part assigned to Mrs. Esmond and the part assigned to the Baroness, to decide if he were short-sighted or ungenerous, if he were inapprehensive or only cruel. They weary easily of his dogged and unremitting pursuit of the merely conventional man and the merely conventional woman; they cannot always bring themselves to be interested in the cupboard drama, the tea-cup tragedies and cheque-book and bandbox comedies, which he regards as the stuff of human action and the web of human life; and from their theory of existence they positively refuse to eliminate the heroic qualities of romance and mystery and passion, which are—as they have only to open their newspapers to see—essentials of human achievement and integral elements of human character. They hold that his books contain some of the finest stuff in fiction: as, for instance, Rawdon Crawley's discovery of his wife and Lord Steyne, and Henry Esmond's return from the wars, and those immortal chapters in which the Colonel and Frank Castlewood pursue and run down their kinswoman and the Prince. But they hold, too, that their influence is dubious, and that few have risen from them one bit the better or one jot the happier.

Which is Right?

Genius apart, Thackeray's morality is that of a highly respectable British cynic; his intelligence is largely one of trifles; he is wise over trivial and trumpery things. He delights in reminding us—with an air!—that everybody is a humbug; that we are all rank snobs; that to misuse your aspirates is to be ridiculous and incapable of real merit; that Miss Blank has just slipped out to post a letter to Captain Jones; that Miss Dash wears false teeth and a wig; that General Tufto is almost as tightly laced as the beautiful Miss Hopper; that there's a bum-bailiff in the kitchen at Number Thirteen; that the dinner we ate t'other day at Timmins's is still to pay; that all is vanity; that there's a skeleton in every house; that passion, enthusiasm, excess of any sort, is unwise, abominable, a little absurd; and so forth. And side by side with these assurances are admirable sketches of character and still more admirable sketches of habit and of manners—are the Pontos and Costigan, Gandish and Talbot Twysden and the unsurpassable Major, Sir Pitt and Brand Firmin, the heroic De la Pluche and the engaging Farintosh and the versatile Honeyman, a crowd of vivid and diverting portraitures besides; but they are not different—in kind at least—from the reflections suggested by the story of their several careers and the development of their several individualities. Esmond apart, there is scarce a man or a woman in Thackeray whom it is possible to love unreservedly or thoroughly respect. That gives the measure of the man, and determines the quality of his influence. He was the average clubman *plus* genius and a style. And, if there is any truth in the theory that it is the function of art not to degrade but to ennoble—not to dishearten but to encourage—not to deal with things ugly and paltry and mean but with great things and beautiful and lofty—then, it is argued, his example is one to depreciate and to condemn.

His Style.

Thus the two sects: the sect of them that are with Thackeray and the sect of them that are against him. Where both agree is in the fact of Thackeray's pre-eminence as a writer of English and the master of one of the finest prose styles in literature. His manner is the perfection of conversational writing. Graceful yet vigorous; adorably artificial yet incomparably sound; touched with modishness yet informed with distinction; easily and happily rhythmical yet full of colour and quick with malice and with meaning; instinct with urbanity and instinct with charm—it is a type of high-bred English, a climax of literary art. He may not have been a great man but assuredly he was a great writer; he may have been a faulty novelist but assuredly he was a rare artist in words. Setting aside Cardinal Newman's, the style he wrote is certainly less open to criticism than that of any other modern Englishman. He was neither super-eloquent like Mr. Ruskin nor a Germanised Jeremy like Carlyle; he was not marmoreally emphatic as Landor was, nor was he slovenly and inexpressive as was the great Sir Walter; he neither dallied with antithesis like Macaulay nor rioted in verbal vulgarisms with Dickens; he abstained from technology and what may be called Lord-Burleighism as carefully as George Eliot indulged in them, and he avoided conceits as sedulously as Mr. George Meredith goes out of his way to hunt for them. He is a better writer than any one of these, in that he is always a master of speech and of himself, and that he is always careful yet natural and choice yet seemingly spontaneous. He wrote as a very prince among talkers, and he interfused and interpenetrated English with the elegant and cultured fashion of the men of Queen Anne and with something of the warmth, the glow, the personal and romantic ambition, peculiar to the century of Byron and Keats, of Landor and Dickens, of Ruskin and Tennyson and Carlyle. Unlike his only rival, he had learnt his art before he began to practise it. Of the early work of the greater artist a good half is that of a man in the throes of education: the ideas, the thoughts, the passion, the poetry, the humour, are of the best, but the expression is self-conscious, strained, ignorant. Thackeray had no such blemish. He wrote dispassionately, and he was a born writer. In him there is no hesitation, no fumbling, no uncertainty. The style of *Barry Lyndon* is better and stronger and more virile than the style of *Philip*; and unlike the other man's, whose latest writing is his best, their author's evolution was towards decay.

His Mission.

He is so superior a person that to catch him tripping is a peculiar pleasure. It is a satisfaction apart, for instance, to reflect that he has (it must be owned) a certain gentility of mind. Like the M.P. in *Martin Chuzzlewit*, he represents the Gentlemanly Interest. That is his mission in literature, and he fulfils it thoroughly. He appears sometimes as Mr. Yellowplush, sometimes as Mr. Fitzboodle, sometimes as Michael Angelo Titmarsh, but always in the Gentlemanly Interest. In his youth (as ever) he is found applauding the well-bred Charles de Bernard, and remarking of Balzac and Dumas that the one is 'not fit for the *salon*,' and the other 'about as genteel as a courier.' Balzac and Dumas are only men of genius and great artists: the real thing is to be 'genteel' and write—as *Gerfeuil* (*sic*) is written—'in a gentleman-like style.' A few pages further on in the same pronouncement (a review of *Jérôme Paturot*), I find him quoting with entire approval Reybaud's sketch of 'a great character, in whom the *habitué* of Paris will perhaps recognise a certain likeness to a certain celebrity of the present day, by name Monsieur Hector Berlioz, the musician and critic.' The description is too long to quote. It sparkles with all the *fadaises* of anti-Berliozian criticism, and the point is that the hero, after conducting at a private party (which Berlioz never did) his own 'hymn of the creation that has been lost since the days of the deluge,' 'called for his cloak and his clogs, and walked home, where he wrote a critique for the newspapers of the music which he had composed and directed.' In the Gentlemanly Interest Mr. Titmarsh translates this sorry little libel with the utmost innocence of approval. It is *The Paris Sketch-Book* over again. That Monsieur Hector Berlioz may possibly have known something of his trade and been withal as honest a man and artist as himself seems never to have occurred to him. He knows nothing of Monsieur Hector except that he is a 'hairy romantic,' and that whatever he wrote it was not *Batti, batti*; but that nothing is enough. 'Whether this little picture is a likeness or not,' he is ingenuous enough to add, 'who shall say?' But,—and here speaks the bold but superior Briton—'it is a good caricature of a race in France, where geniuses *poussent* as they do nowhere else; where poets are prophets, where romances have revelations.' As he goes on to qualify *Jérôme Paturot* as a 'masterpiece,' and as 'three volumes of satire in which there is not a particle of bad blood,' it seems fair to conclude that in the Gentlemanly Interest all is considered fair, and that to accuse a man of writing criticisms on his own works is to be 'witty and entertaining,' and likewise 'careless, familiar, and sparkling' to the genteelest purpose possible in this genteelest of all possible worlds.

DISRAELI

His Novels.

To the general his novels must always be a kind of caviare; for they have no analogue in letters, but are the output of a mind and temper of singular originality. To the honest Tory, sworn to admire and unable to comprehend, they must seem inexplicable as abnormal. To the professional Radical they are so many proofs of innate inferiority: for they are full of pretentiousness and affectation; they teem with examples of all manner of vices, from false English to an immoral delight in dukes; they prove their maker a trickster and a charlatan in every page. To them, however, whose first care is for rare work, the series of novels that began with *Vivian Grey* and ended with *Endymion* is one of the pleasant facts in modern letters. These books abound in wit and daring, in originality and shrewdness, in knowledge of the world and in knowledge of men; they contain many vivid and striking studies of character, both portrait and caricature; they sparkle with speaking phrases and happy epithets; they are aglow with the passion of youth, the love of love, the worship of physical beauty, the admiration of whatever is costly and select and splendid—from a countess to a castle, from a duke to a diamond; they are radiant with delight in whatever is powerful or personal or attractive—from a cook to a cardinal, from an agitator to an emperor. They often remind you of Voltaire, often of Balzac, often of *The Arabian Nights*. You pass from an heroic drinking bout to a brilliant criticism of style; from rhapsodies on bands and ortolans that remind you of Heine to a gambling scene that for directness and intensity may vie with the bluntest and strongest work of Prosper Mérimée; from the extravagant impudence of *Popanilla* to the sentimental rodomontade of *Henrietta Temple*; from ranting romanticism in *Alroy* to vivid realism in *Sybil*. Their author gives you no time to weary of him, for he is worldly and passionate, fantastic and trenchant, cynical and ambitious, flippant and sentimental, ornately rhetorical and triumphantly simple in a breath. He is imperiously egoistic, but while constantly parading his own personality he is careful never to tell you anything about it. And withal he is imperturbably good-tempered: he brands and gibbets with a smile, and with a smile he adores and applauds. Intellectually he is in sympathy with character of every sort; he writes as becomes an artist who has recognised that 'the conduct of men depends upon the temperament, not upon a bunch of musty maxims,' and that 'there is a great deal of vice that is really sheer inadvertence.' It is said that the Monmouth of *Coningsby* and the Steyne of *Vanity Fair* are painted from one and the same original; and you have but to compare the savage realism of Thackeray's study to the scornful amenity of the other's—as you have but to contrast the elaborate and extravagant cruelty of Thackeray's Alcide de Mirobolant with the polite and half-respectful irony of Disraeli's treatment of the cooks in *Tancred*—to perceive that in certain ways the advantage is not with 'the greatest novelist of his time,' and that the Monmouth produces an impression which is more moral because more kindly and humane than the impression left by the Steyne, while in its way it is every whit as vivid and as convincing. Yet another excellence, and a great one, is his mastery of apt and forcible dialogue. The talk of Mr. Henry James's personages is charmingly equable and appropriate, but it is also trivial and tame; the talk in Anthony Trollope is surprisingly natural and abundant, but it is also commonplace and immemorable; the talk of Mr. George Meredith is always eloquent and fanciful, but the eloquence is too often dark and the fancy too commonly inhuman. What Disraeli's people have to say is not always original nor profound, but it is crisply and happily phrased and uttered, it reads well, its impression seldom fails of permanency. His *Wit and Wisdom* is a kind of *Talker's Guide* or *Handbook of Conversation*. How should it be otherwise, seeing that it contains the characteristic utterances of a great artist in life renowned for memorable speech?

A Contrast.

Now, if you ask a worshipper of him that was so long his rival, to repeat a saying, a maxim, a sentence, of which his idol is the author, it is odds but he will look like a fool, and visit you with an evasive answer. What else should he do? His deity is a man of many words and no sayings. He is the prince of agitators, but it would be impossible for him to mint a definition of 'agitation'; he is the world's most eloquent arithmetician, but it is beyond him to epigrammatise the fact that two and two make four. And it seems certain, unless the study of Homer and religious fiction inspire him to some purpose, that his contributions to axiomatic literature will be still restricted to the remark that 'There are three courses open' to something or other: to the House, to the angry cabman, to what and whomsoever you will. In sober truth, he is one who writes for to-day, and takes no thought of either yesterdays or morrows. For him the Future is next session; the Past does not extend beyond his last change of mind. He is a prince of journalists, and his excursions into monthly literature remain to show how great and copious a master of the 'leader'—ornate, imposing, absolutely insignificant—his absorption in politics has cost the English-speaking world.

His Backgrounds.

Disraeli's imagination, at once practical and extravagant, is not of the kind that delights in plot and counterplot. His novels abound in action, but the episodes wear a more or less random look: the impression produced is pretty much that of a story of adventure. But if they fail as stories they are unexceptionable as canvases. Our author unrolls them with superb audacity; and rapidly and vigorously he fills them in with places and people, with faces that are as life and words expressive even as they. Nothing is too lofty or too low for him. He hawks at every sort of game, and rarely does he make a false cast. It is but a step from the wilds of Lancashire to the Arabian Desert, from the cook's first floor to the Home of the Bellamonts; for he has the Seven-League-Boots of the legend, and more than the genius of adventure of him that wore them. His castles may be of cardboard, his cataracts of tinfoil, the sun of his adjurations the veriest figment; but he never lets his readers see that he knows it. His irony, sudden and reckless and insidious though it be, yet never extends to his properties. There may be a sneer beneath that mask which, with an egotism baffling as imperturbable, he delights in intruding among his creations; but you cannot see it. You suspect its presence, because he is a born mocker. But you remember that one of his most obvious idiosyncrasies is an inordinate love of all that is sumptuous, glittering, radiant, magnificent; and you incline to suspect that he keeps his sneering for the world of men, and admires his scenes and decorations too cordially to visit them with anything so merciless.

His Men and Women.

But dashing and brilliant as are his sketches of places and things, they are after all the merest accessories. It was as a student of Men and Women that he loved to excel, and it is as their painter that I praise him now. Himself a worshipper of intellect, it was intellectually that he mastered and developed them. Like Sidonia he moves among them not to feel with them but to understand and learn from them. Such sympathy as he had was either purely sensuous, as for youth and beauty and all kinds of comeliness; or purely intellectual, as for intelligence, artificiality, servility, meanness. And as his essence was satirical, as he was naturally irreverent and contemptuous, it follows that he is best and strongest in the act of punishment not of reward. His passion for youth was beautiful, but it did not make him strong. His scorn for things contemptible, his hate for things hateful, are at times too bitter even for those who think with him; but in these lay his force—they filled his brain with light, and they touched his lips with fire. The wretched Rigby is far more vigorous and life-like than the amiable Coningsby;

Views and Reviews

Tom Cogit—a sketch, but a sketch of genius—is infinitely more interesting than May Dacre or even the Young Duke; Tancred is a good fellow, and very real and true in his goodness, but contrast him with Fakredeen! And after his knaves, his fools, his tricksters, the most striking figures in his gallery are those whom he has considered from a purely intellectual point of view: either kindly, as Sidonia, or coolly, as Lord Monmouth, but always calmly and with no point of passion in his regard: the Eskdales, Villebecques, Ormsbys, Bessos, Marneys, Meltons, and Mirabels, the Bohuns and St. Aldegondes and Grandisons, the Tadpoles and the Tapers, the dominant and subaltern humanity of the world. All these are drawn with peculiar boldness of line, precision of touch, and clearness of intention. And as with his men so is it with his women: the finest are not those he likes best but those who interested him most. Male and female, his eccentrics surpass his commonplaces. He had a great regard for girls, and his attitude towards them, or such of them as he elected heroines, was mostly one of adoration—magnificent yet a little awkward and strained. With women, married women, he had vastly more in common: he could admire, study, divine, without having to feign a warmer feeling; and while his girls are poor albeit splendid young persons, his matrons are usually delightful. Edith Millbank is not a very striking figure in *Coningsby*; but her appearance in *Tancred*—well, you have only to compare it to the resurrection of Laura Bell, as Mrs. Pendennis to see how good it is.

His Style.

Now and then the writing is bad, and the thought is stale. Disraeli had many mannerisms, innate and acquired. His English was frequently loose and inexpressive; he was apt to trip in his grammar, to stumble over 'and which,' and to be careless about the connection between his nominatives and his verbs. Again, he could scarce ever refrain from the use of gorgeous commonplaces of sentiment and diction. His taste was sometimes ornately and barbarically conventional; he wrote as an orator, and his phrases often read as if he had used them for the sake of their associations rather than themselves. His works are a casket of such stage jewels of expression as 'Palladian structure,' 'Tusculan repose,' 'Gothic pile,' 'pellucid brow,' 'mossy cell,' and 'dew-bespangled meads.' He delighted in 'hyacinthine curls' and 'lustrous locks,' in 'smiling parterres' and 'stately terraces.' He seldom sat down in print to anything less than a 'banquet', he was capable of invoking 'the iris pencil of Hope'; he could not think nor speak of the beauties of woman except as 'charms.' Which seems to show that to be 'born in a library,' and have Voltaire—that impeccable master of the phrase—for your chief of early heroes and exemplars is not everything.

Views and Reviews

His Oratory.

It is admitted, I believe, that he had many of the qualities of a great public speaker: that he had an admirable voice and an excellent method; that his sequences were logical and natural, his arguments vigorous and persuasive; that he was an artist in style, and in the course of a single speech could be eloquent and vivacious, ornate and familiar, passionate and cynical, deliberately rhetorical and magnificently fantastic in turn; that he was a master of all oratorical modes—of irony and argument, of stately declamation and brilliant and unexpected antithesis, of caricature and statement and rejoinder alike; that he could explain, denounce, retort, retract, advance, defy, dispute, with equal readiness and equal skill; that he was unrivalled in attack and unsurpassed in defence; and that in heated debate and on occasions when he felt himself justified in putting forth all his powers and in striking in with the full weight of his imperious and unique personality he was the most dangerous antagonist of his time. And yet, in spite of his mysterious and commanding influence over his followers—in spite, too, of the fact that he died assuredly the most romantic and perhaps the most popular figure of his time—it is admitted withal that he was lacking in a certain quality of temperament, that attribute great orators possess in common with great actors: the power, that is, of imposing oneself upon an audience not by argument nor by eloquence, not by the perfect utterance of beautiful and commanding speech nor by the enunciation of eternal principles or sympathetic and stirring appeals, but by an effect of personal magnetism, by the expression through voice and gesture and presence of an individuality, a temperament, call it what you will, that may be and is often utterly commonplace but is always inevitably irresistible. He could slaughter an opponent, or butcher a measure, or crumple up a theory with unrivalled adroitness and despatch; but he could not dominate a crowd to the extent of persuading it to feel with his heart, think with his brain, and accept his utterances as the expression not only of their common reason but of their collective sentiment as well. He was as incapable of such a feat as Mr. Gladstone's Midlothian campaign as Mr. Gladstone is of producing the gaming scene in *The Young Duke* or the 'exhausted volcanoes' paragraph in the Manchester speech.

His Speeches as Literature.

As a rule—a rule to which there are some magnificent exceptions—orators have only to cease from speaking to become uninteresting. What has been heard with enthusiasm is read with indifference or even with astonishment. You miss the noble voice, the persuasive gesture, the irresistible personality; and with the emotional faculty at rest and the reason at work you are surprised—and it may be a little indignant—that you should have been impressed so deeply as you were by such cold, bald verbosity as seen in black and white the masterpiece of yesterday appears to be. To some extent this is the case with these speeches of Disraeli's. At the height of debate, amid the clash of personal and party animosities, with the cheers of the orator's supporters to give them wings, they sounded greater than they were. But for all that they are vigorous and profitable yet. Their author's unfailing capacity for saying things worth heeding and remembering is proved in every one of them. It is not easy to open either of Mr. Kebbel's volumes without lighting upon something—a string of epigrams, a polished gibe, a burst of rhetoric, an effective collocation of words—that proclaims the artist. In this connection the perorations are especially instructive, even if you consider them simply as arrangements of sonorous and suggestive words: as oratorical impressions carefully prepared, as effects of what may be called vocalised orchestration touched off as skilfully and with as fine a sense of sound and of the sentiment to correspond as so many passages of instrumentation signed 'Berlioz' might be.

The Great Earl.

Fruits fail, and love dies, and time ranges; and only the whippersnapper (that fool of Time) endureth for ever.

Molière knew him well, and he said that Molière was a liar and a thief. And Disraeli knew him too, and he said that in these respects Disraeli and Molière were brothers. That he said so matters as little now as ever it did; for though the whippersnapper is immortal in kind, he is nothing if not futile and ephemeral in effect, and it was seen long since that in life and death Disraeli, as became his genius and his race, was the Uncommonplace incarnate, the antithesis of Grocerdom, the Satan of that revolt against the yielding habit of Jehovah-Bottles the spirit whereof is fast coming to be our one defence against socialism and the dominion of the Common Fool. He was no sentimentalist: as what great artist in government has ever been? He loved power for power's sake, and recognising to the full the law of the survival of the fittest he preferred his England to the world. He knew that it is the function of the man of genius to show that theory is only theory, and that in the House of Morality there are many mansions. To that end he lived and died; and it is not until one has comprehended the complete significance of his life and death that one is qualified to speak with understanding of such a life and death as his who passed at Khartoum.

ALEXANDRE DUMAS

His Components.

The life of Dumas is not only a monument of endeavour and success, it is a sort of labyrinth as well. It abounds in pseudonyms and disguises, in sudden and unexpected appearances and retreats as unexpected and sudden, in scandals and in rumours, in mysteries and traps and ambuscades of every kind. It pleased the great man to consider himself of more importance than any and all of the crowd of collaborators whose ideas he developed, whose raw material he wrought up into the achievement we know; and he was given to take credit to himself not only for the success and value of a particular work but for the whole thing—the work in its quiddity, so to speak, and resolved into its original elements. On the other hand, it pleased such painful creatures as MM. Quérard and 'Eugène de Mirecourt,' as it has since pleased Messrs. Hitchman and Fitzgerald to consider the second- and third-rate literary persons whom Dumas assimilated in such numbers as of greater interest and higher merit than Dumas. To them the jackals were far nobler than the lion, and they worked their hardest in the interest of the pack. It was their mission to decompose and disintegrate the magnificent entity which M. Blaze de Bury very happily nicknames 'Dumas-Légion,' and in the process not to render his own unto Cæsar but to take from him all that was Cæsar's, and divide it among the mannikins he had absorbed. And their work was in its way well done; for have we not seen M. Brunetière exulting in agreement and talking of Dumas as one less than Eugène Sue and not much bigger than Gaillardet? Of course the ultimate issue of the debate is not doubtful. Dumas remains to the end a prodigy of force and industry, a miracle of cleverness and accomplishment and ease, a type of generous and abundant humanity, a great artist in many varieties of form, a prince of talkers and story-tellers, one of the kings of the stage, a benefactor of his epoch and his kind; while of those who assisted him in the production of his immense achievement the most exist but as fractions of the larger sum, and the others have utterly disappeared. 'Combien,' says his son in that excellent page which serves to preface *le Fils Naturel*—'combien parmi ceux qui devaient rester obscurs se sont éclairés et chauffés à ta forge, et si l'heure des restitutions sonnait, quel gain pour toi, rien qu'à reprendre ce que tu as donné et ce qu'on t'a pris!' That is the true verdict of posterity, and he does well who abides by it.

Views and Reviews

Himself.

He is one of the heroes of modern art. Envy and scandal have done their worst now. The libeller has said his say; the detectives who make a specialty of literary forgeries have proved their cases one and all; the judges of matter have spoken, and so have the critics of style; the distinguished author of *Nana* has taken us into his confidence on the subject; we have heard from the lamented Granier and others as much as was to be heard on the question of plagiarism in general and the plagiarisms of Dumas in particular; and Mr. Percy Fitzgerald has done what he is pleased to designate the 'nightman's work' of analysing *Antony* and *Kean*, and of collecting everything that spite has said about their author's life, their author's habits, their author's manners and customs and character: of whose vanity, mendacity, immorality, a score of improper qualities besides, enough has been written to furnish a good-sized library. And the result of it all is that Dumas is recognised for a force in modern art and for one of the greatest inventors and amusers the century has produced. Whole crowds of men were named as the real authors of his books and plays; but they were only readable when he signed for them. His ideas were traced to a hundred originals; but they had all seemed worthless till he took them in hand and developed them according to their innate capacity. The French he wrote was popular, and the style at his command was none of the loftiest, as his critics have often been at pains to show; but he was for all that an artist at once original and exemplary, with an incomparable instinct of selection, a constructive faculty not equalled among the men of this century, an understanding of what is right and what is wrong in art and a mastery of his materials which in their way are not to be paralleled in the work of Sir Walter himself. Like Napoleon, he was 'a natural force let loose'; and if he had done no more than achieve universal renown as the prince of *raconteurs* and a commanding position as a novelist wherever novels are read he would still have done much. But he did a vast deal more. A natural force, he wrought in the right direction, as natural forces must and do. He amused the world for forty years and more; but he also contributed something to the general sum of the world's artistic experience and capacity, and his contribution is of permanent worth and charm. He has left us stories which are models of the enchanting art of narrative; and, with a definition good and comprehensive enough to include all the best work which has been produced for the theatre from Æschylus down to Augier, from the *Choephoræ* on to *le Gendre de M. Poirier,* he has given us types of the romantic and the domestic drama, which, new when he produced them, are even now not old, and which as regards essentials have yet to be improved upon. The form and aim of the modern drama, as we know it, have been often enough ascribed to the ingenious author of *une Chaîne* and the *Verre d'Eau*; but they might with much greater truth be ascribed to the author of *Antony* and *la Tour de Nesle*. Scribe invents and eludes where Dumas invents and dares. The theory of Scribe is one of mere dexterity: his drama is a perpetual *chassé-croisé* at the edge of a precipice, a dance of puppets among swords that might but will not cut and eggs that might but will not break; to him a situation is a kind of tight-rope to be crossed with ever so much agility and an endless affectation of peril by all his characters in turn: in fact, as M. Dumas *fils* has said of him, he is 'le Shakespeare des ombres chinoises.' The theory of Dumas is the very antipodes of this. 'All I want,' he said in a memorable comparison between himself and Victor Hugo, 'is four trestles, four boards, two actors, and a passion'; and his good plays are a proof that in this he spoke no more than the truth. Drama to him was so much emotion in action. If he invented a situation he accepted its issues in their entirety, and did his utmost to express from it all the passion it contained. That he fails to reach the highest peaks of emotional effect is no fault of his: to do that something more is needed than a perfect method, something other than a great ambition and an absolute certainty of touch; and Dumas was neither a Shakespeare nor an Æschylus—he was not even an Augier. All the same, he has produced in *la Tour de Nesle* a romantic play which M. Zola himself pronounces the ideal of the *genre* and in *Antony* an achievement in drawing-room tragedy which is out of all questioning the first, and in the opinion of a critic so competent and so keen as the master's son is probably the strongest, thing of its kind in modern literature. On this latter play it were difficult, I think, to bestow too much attention. It is touched, even tainted, with the manner and the affectation of its epoch. But it is admirably imagined and contrived; it is very daring, and it is very new; it deals with the men and women of 1830, and—with due allowance for differences of manners, ideal, and personal genius—it is in its essentials a play in the same sense as *Othello* and the *Trachiniæ* are plays in theirs. It is the beginning, as I believe, not only of *les Lionnes Pauvres* but of *Thérèse Raquin* and *la Glu* as well: just as *la Tour de Nesle* is the beginning of *Patrie* and *la Haine*.

At Least.

And if these greater and loftier pretensions be still contested; if the theory of the gifted creature who wrote that the works of the master wizard are 'like summer fruits brought forth abundantly in the full blaze of sunshine, which do not keep'—if this preposterous fantasy be generally accepted, there will yet be much in Dumas to venerate and love. If *Antony* were of no more account than an ephemeral burlesque; if *la Reine Margot* and the immortal trilogy of the Musketeers—that 'epic of friendship'—were dead as morality and as literature alike; if it were nothing to have recast the novel of adventure, formulated the modern drama, and perfected the drama of incident; if to have sent all France to the theatre to see in three dimensions those stories of Chicot, Edmond Dantès, d'Artagnan, which it knew by heart from books were an achievement within the reach of every scribbler who dabbles in letters; if all this were true, and Dumas were merely a piece of human journalism, produced to-day and gone to-morrow, there would still be enough of him to make his a memorable name. He was a prodigy—of amiability, cleverness, energy, daring, charm, industry—if he was nothing else. Gronow tells that he has sat at table with Dumas and Brougham, and that Brougham, out-faced and out-talked, was forced to quit the field. 'J'ai conservé,' says M. Maxime du Camp, in his admirable *Souvenirs littéraires*, 'd'Alexandre Dumas un souvenir ineffaçable; malgré un certain laisser-aller qui tenait à l'exubérance de sa nature, c'était un homme *dont tous les sentiments étaient élevés*. On a été injuste pour lui; comme il avait énormément d'esprit, on l'a accusé d'être léger; comme il produisait avec une facilité incroyable, on l'a accusé de gâcher la besogne, et, comme il était prodigue, on l'a accusé de manquer de tenue. Ces reproches m'ont toujours paru misérables.' This is much; but it is not nearly all. He had, this independent witness goes on to note, 'une générosité naturelle qui ne comptait jamais; il ressemblait à une corne d'abondance qui se vide sans cesse dans les mains tendues; *la moitié, sinon plus, de l'argent gagné par lui a été donnée.*' That is true; and it is also true that he gave at least as largely of himself—his prodigious temperament, his generous gaiety, his big, manly heart, his turn for chivalry, his gallant and delightful genius—as of his money. He was reputed a violent and luxurious debauchee; and he mostly lived in an attic—(the worst room in the house and therefore the only one he could call his own)—with a camp-bed and the deal table at which he wrote. He passed for a loud-mouthed idler; and during many years his daily average of work was fourteen hours for months on end. 'Ivre de puissance,' says George Sand of him, but 'foncièrement bon.' They used to hear him laughing as he wrote, and when he killed Porthos he did no more that day. It would have been worth while to figure as one of the crowd of friends and parasites who lived at rack and manger in his house, for the mere pleasure of seeing him descend upon them from his toil of moving mountains and sharing in that pleasing half-hour of talk which was his common refreshment. After that he would return to the attic and the deal table, and move more mountains. With intervals of travel, sport, adventure, and what in France is called 'l'amour'—(it is strange, by the way, that he was never a hero of Carlyle's)—he lived in this way more or less for forty years or so; and when he left Paris for the last time he had but two napoleons in his pocket. 'I had only one when I came here first,' quoth he, 'and yet they call me a spendthrift.' That was his way; and while the result is not for Dr. Smiles to chronicle, I for one persist in regarding the spirit in which it was accepted as not less exemplary than delightful.

His Monument.

On M. du Camp's authority there is a charming touch to add to his son's description of him. 'Il me semble,' said the royal old prodigal in his last illness, 'que je suis au sommet d'un monument qui tremble comme si les fondations étaient assises sur le sable.' 'Sois en paix,' replied the author of the *Demi-Monde*: 'le monument est bien bati, et la base est solide.' He was right, as we know. It is good and fitting that Dumas should have a monument in the Paris he amazed and delighted and amused so long. But he could have done without one. In what language is he not read? and where that he is read is he not loved? '*Exegi monumentum*,' he might have said: 'and wherever romance is a necessary of life, there shall you look for it, and not in vain.'

GEORGE MEREDITH

His Qualities.

To read Mr. Meredith's novels with insight is to find them full of the rarest qualities in fiction. If their author has a great capacity for unsatisfactory writing he has capacities not less great for writing that is satisfactory in the highest degree. He has the tragic instinct and endowment, and he has the comic as well; he is an ardent student of character and life; he has wit of the swiftest, the most comprehensive, the most luminous, and humour that can be fantastic or ironical or human at his pleasure; he has passion and he has imagination; he has considered sex—the great subject, the leaven of imaginative art—with notable audacity and insight. He is as capable of handling a vice or an emotion as he is of managing an affectation. He can be trivial, or grotesque, or satirical, or splendid; and whether his *milieu* be romantic or actual, whether his personages be heroic or sordid, he goes about his task with the same assurance and intelligence. In his best work he takes rank with the world's novelists. He is a companion for Balzac and Richardson, an intimate for Fielding and Cervantes. His figures fall into their place beside the greatest of their kind; and when you think of Lucy Feverel and Mrs. Berry, of Evan Harrington's

Countess Saldanha and the Lady Charlotte of *Emilia in England*, of the two old men in *Harry Richmond* and the Sir Everard Romfrey of *Beauchamp's Career*, of Renée and Cecilia, of Emilia and Rhoda Fleming, of Rose Jocelyn and Lady Blandish and Ripton Thompson, they have in the mind's eye a value scarce inferior to that of Clarissa and Lovelace, of Bath and Western and Booth, of Andrew Fairservice and Elspeth Mucklebacket, of Philippe Bridau and Vautrin and Balthasar Claës. In the world of man's creation his people are citizens to match the noblest; they are of the aristocracy of the imagination, the peers in their own right of the society of romance. And for all that, their state is mostly desolate and lonely and forlorn.

His Defects.

For Mr. Meredith is one of the worst and least attractive of great writers as well as one of the best and most fascinating. He is a sun that has broken out into innumerable spots. The better half of his genius is always suffering eclipse from the worse half. He writes with the pen of a great artist in his left hand and the razor of a spiritual suicide in his right. He is the master and the victim of a monstrous cleverness which is neither to hold nor to bind, and will not permit him to do things as an honest, simple person of genius would. As Shakespeare, in Johnson's phrase, lost the world for a quibble and was content to lose it, so does Mr. Meredith discrown himself of the sovereignty of contemporary romance to put on the cap and bells of the professional wit. He is not content to be plain Jupiter: his lightnings are less to him than his fireworks; and his pages so teem with fine sayings and magniloquent epigrams and gorgeous images and fantastic locutions that the mind would welcome dulness as a bright relief. He is tediously amusing; he is brilliant to the point of being obscure; his helpfulness is so extravagant as to worry and confound. That is the secret of his unpopularity. His stories are not often good stories and are seldom well told; his ingenuity and intelligence are always misleading him into treating mere episodes as solemnly and elaborately as main incidents; he is ever ready to discuss, to ramble, to theorise, to dogmatise, to indulge in a little irony or a little reflection or a little artistic misdemeanour of some sort. But other novelists have done these things before him, and have been none the less popular, and are actually none the less readable. None, however, has pushed the foppery of style and intellect to such a point as Mr. Meredith. Not infrequently he writes page after page of English as ripe and sound and unaffected as heart could wish; and you can but impute to wantonness and recklessness the splendid impertinences that intrude elsewhere. To read him at the rate of two or three chapters a day is to have a sincere and hearty admiration for him and a devout anxiety to forget his defects and make much of his merits. But they are few who can take a novel on such terms as these, and to read your Meredith straight off is to have an indigestion of epigram, and to be incapable of distinguishing good from bad: the author of the parting between Richard and Lucy Feverel—a high-water mark of novelistic passion and emotion—from the creator of Mr. Raikes and Dr. Shrapnel, which are two of the most flagrant unrealities ever perpetrated in the name of fiction by an artist of genius.

Another Way.

On the whole, I think, he does not often say anything not worth hearing. He is too wise for that; and, besides, he is strenuously in earnest about his work. He has a noble sense of the dignity of art and the responsibilities of the artist; he will set down nothing that is to his mind unworthy to be recorded; his treatment of his material is distinguished by the presence of an intellectual passion (as it were) that makes whatever he does considerable and deserving of attention and respect. But unhappily the will is not seldom unequal to the deed: the achievement is often leagues in rear of the inspiration; the attempt at completeness is too laboured and too manifest—the feat is done but by a painful and ungraceful process. There *is* genius, but there is *not* felicity: that, one is inclined to say, is the distinguishing note of Mr. Meredith's work, in prose and verse alike. There are magnificent exceptions, of course, but they prove the rule and, broken though it be, there is no gainsaying its existence. To be concentrated in form, to be suggestive in material, to say nothing that is not of permanent value, and only to say it in such terms as are charged to the fullest with significance—this would seem to be the aim and end of Mr. Meredith's ambition. Of simplicity in his own person he appears incapable. The texture of his expression must be stiff with allusion, or he deems it ill spun; there must be something of antic in his speech, or he cannot believe he is addressing himself to the Immortals; he has praised with perfect understanding the lucidity, the elegance, the ease, of Molière, and yet his aim in art (it would appear) is to be Molière's antipodes, and to vanquish by congestion, clottedness, an anxious and determined dandyism of form and style. There is something *bourgeois* in his intolerance of the commonplace, something fanatical in the intemperance of his regard for artifice. 'Le dandy,' says Baudelaire, 'doit aspirer à être sublime sans interruption. Il doit vivre et dormir devant un miroir.' That, you are tempted to believe, is Mr. Meredith's theory of expression. 'Ce qu'il y a dans le mauvais goût,' is elsewhere the opinion of the same unamiable artist in paradox, 'c'est le plaisir aristocratique de déplaire.' Is that, you ask yourself, the reason why Mr. Meredith is so contemptuous of the general public?—why he will stoop to no sort of concession nor permit himself a mite of patience with the herd whose intellect is content with such poor fodder as Scott and Dickens and Dumas? Be it as it may, the effect is the same. Our author is bent upon being 'uninterruptedly sublime'; and we must take him as he wills and as we find him. He loses of course; and we suffer. But none the less do we cherish his society, and none the less are we interested in his processes, and enchanted (when we are clever enough) by his results. He lacks felicity, I have said; but he has charm as well as power, and, once his rule is accepted, there is no way to shake him off. The position is that of the antique tyrant in a commonwealth once republican and free. You resent the domination, but you enjoy it too, and with or against your will you admire the author of your slavery.

Rhoda Fleming.

Rhoda Fleming is one of the least known of the novels, and in a sense it is one of the most disagreeable. To the general it has always been caviare, and caviare it is likely to remain; for the general is before all things respectable, and no such savage and scathing attack upon the superstitions of respectability as *Rhoda Fleming* has been written. And besides, the emotions developed are too tragic, the personages too elementary in kind and too powerful in degree, the effects too poignant and too sorrowful. In these days people read to be amused. They care for no passion that is not decent in itself and whose expression is not restrained. It irks them to grapple with problems capable of none save a tragic solution. And when Mr. Meredith goes digging in a very bad temper with things in general into the deeper strata, the primitive deposits, of human nature, the public is the reverse of profoundly interested in the outcome of his exploration and the results of his labour. But for them whose eye is for real literature and such literary essentials as character largely seen and largely presented and as passion deeply felt and poignantly expressed there is such a feast in *Rhoda Fleming* as no other English novelist alive has spread. The book, it is true, is full of failures. There is, for instance, the old bank porter Anthony, who is such a failure as only a great novelist may perpetrate and survive; who suggests (with some other of Mr. Meredith's creations) a close, deliberate, and completely unsuccessful imitation of Dickens: a writer with whom Mr. Meredith is not averse from entering into competition, and who, so manifest on these occasions is his superiority, may almost be described as the other's evil genius. Again, there is Algernon the fool, of whom his author is so bitterly contemptuous that he is never once permitted to live and move and have any sort of being whatever and who, though he bears a principal part in the intrigue, like the Blifil of *Tom Jones* is so constantly illuminated by the lightnings of the ironical mode of presentation as always to seem unreal in himself and seriously to imperil the reality of the story. And, lastly, there are the chivalrous Percy Waring and the inscrutable Mrs. Lovell, two gentle ghosts whose proper place is the shadow-land of the American novel. But when all these are removed (and for the judicious reader their removal is far from difficult) a treasure of reality remains. What an intensity of life it is that hurries and throbs and burns through the veins of the two sisters—Dahlia the victim, Rhoda the executioner! Where else in English fiction is such a 'human oak log' as their father, the Kentish yeoman William Fleming? And where in English fiction is such a problem presented as that in the evolution of which these three—with a following so well selected and achieved as Robert Armstrong and Jonathan Eccles and the evil ruffian Sedgett, a type of the bumpkin gone wrong, and Master Gammon, that type of the bumpkin old and obstinate, a sort of human saurian—are dashed together, and ground against each other till the weakest and best of the three is broken to pieces? Mr. Meredith may and does fail conspicuously to interest you in Anthony Hackbut and Algernon Blancove and Percy Waring; but he knows every fibre of the rest, and he makes your knowledge as intimate and comprehensive as his own. With these he is never at fault and never out of touch. They have the unity of effect, the vigorous simplicity, of life that belong to great creative art; and at their highest stress of emotion, the culmination of their passion, they appeal to and affect you with a force and a directness that suggest the highest achievement of Webster. Of course this sounds excessive. The expression of human feeling in the coil of a tragic situation is not a characteristic of modern fiction. It is thought to be not consistent with the theory and practice of realism; and the average novelist is afraid of it, the average reader is only affected by it when he goes to look for it in poetry. But the book is there to show that such praise is deserved; and they who doubt it have only to read the chapters called respectively 'When the Night is Darkest' and 'Dahlia's Frenzy' to be convinced and doubt no longer. It has been objected to the climax of *Rhoda Fleming* that it is unnecessarily inhumane, and that Dahlia dead were better art than Dahlia living and incapable of love and joy. But the book, as I have said, is a merciless impeachment of respectability; and as the spectacle of a ruined and broken life is infinitely more discomforting than that of a noble death, I take it that Mr. Meredith was right to prefer his present ending to the alternative, inasmuch as the painfulness of that impression he wished to produce and the potency of that moral he chose to draw are immensely heightened and strengthened thereby.

The Tragic Comedians.

Opinions differ, and there are those, I believe, to whom Alvan and Clotilde von Rüdiger—'acrobats of the affections' they have been called—are pleasant companions, and the story of those feats in the gymnastics of sentimentalism in which they lived to shine is the prettiest reading imaginable. But others not so fortunate or, to be plain, more honestly obtuse persist in finding that story tedious, and the bewildering appearances it deals with not human beings—not of the stock of Rose Jocelyn and Sir Everard Romfrey, of Dahlia Fleming and Lucy Feverel and Richmond Roy—but creatures of gossamer and rainbow, phantasms of spiritual romance, abstractions of remote, dispiriting points in sexual philosophy.

The Egoist.

Just as Molière in the figures of Alceste and Tartuffe has summarised and embodied all that we need to know of indignant honesty and the false fervour of sanctimonious animalism, so in the person of Sir Willoughby Patterne has Mr. Meredith succeeded in expressing the qualities of egoism as the egoist appears in his relations with women and in his conception and exercise of the passion of love. Between the means of the two men there is not, nor can be, any sort of comparison. Molière is brief, exquisite, lucid: classic in his union of ease and strength, of purity and sufficiency, of austerity and charm. In *The Egoist* Mr. Meredith is even more artificial and affected than his wont: he bristles with allusions, he teems with hints and side-hits and false alarms, he glitters with phrases, he riots in intellectual points and philosophical fancies; and though his style does nowhere else become him so well, his cleverness is yet so reckless and indomitable as to be almost as fatiguing here as everywhere. But in their matter the great Frenchman and he have not much to envy each other. Sir Willoughby Patterne is a 'document on humanity' of the highest value; and to him that would know of egoism and the egoist the study of Sir Willoughby is indispensable. There is something in him of us all. He is a compendium of the Personal in man; and if in him the abstract Egoist have not taken on his final shape and become classic and typical it is not that Mr. Meredith has forgotten anything in his composition but rather that there are certain defects of form, certain structural faults and weaknesses, which prevent you from accepting as conclusive the aspect of the mass of him. But the Molière of the future (if the future be that fortunate) has but to pick and choose with discretion here to find the stuff of a companion figure to Arnolphe and Alceste and Célimène.

In Metre.

His verse has all the faults and only some of the merits of his prose. Thus he will rhyme you off a ballad, and to break the secret of that ballad you have to take to yourself a dark lantern and a case of jemmies. I like him best in *The Nuptials of Attila*. If he always wrote as here, and were always as here sustained in inspiration, rapid of march, nervous of phrase, apt of metaphor, and moving in effect, he would be delightful to the general, and that without sacrificing on the vile and filthy altar of popularity. Here he is successfully himself, and what more is there to say? You clap for Harlequin, and you kneel to Apollo. Mr. Meredith doubles the parts, and is irresistible in both. Such fire, such vision, such energy on the one hand and on the other such agility and athletic grace are not often found in combination.

The Fashion of Art.

This is the merit and distinction of art: to be more real than reality, to be not nature but nature's essence. It is the artist's function not to copy but to synthesise: to eliminate from that gross confusion of actuality which is his raw material whatever is accidental, idle, irrelevant, and select for perpetuation that only which is appropriate and immortal. Always artistic, Mr. Meredith's work is often great art.

BYRON

Byron and the World.

Two obvious reasons why Byron has long been a prophet more honoured abroad than at home are his life and his work. He is the most romantic figure in the literature of the century, and his romance is of that splendid and daring cast which the people of Britain—'an aristocracy materialised and null, a middle class purblind and hideous, a lower class crude and brutal'—prefers to regard with suspicion and disfavour. He is the type of them that prove in defiance of precept that the safest path is not always midway, and that the golden rule is sometimes unspeakably worthless: who set what seems a horrible example, create an apparently shameful precedent, and yet contrive to approve themselves an honour to their country and the race. To be a good Briton a man must trade profitably, marry respectably, live cleanly, avoid excess, revere the established order, and wear his heart in his breeches pocket or anywhere but on his sleeve. Byron did none of these things, though he was a public character, and ought for the example's sake to have done them all, and done them ostentatiously. He lived hard, and drank hard, and played hard. He was flippant in speech and eccentric in attire. He thought little of the sanctity of the conjugal tie, and said so; and he married but to divide from his wife—who was an incarnation of the national virtue of respectability—under circumstances too mysterious not to be discreditable. He was hooted into exile, and so far from reforming he did even worse than he had done before. After bewildering Venice with his wickedness and consorting with atheists like Shelley and conspirators like young Gamba, he went away on a sort of wild-goose chase to Greece, and died there with every circumstance of publicity. Also his work was every whit as abominable in the eyes of his countrymen as his life. It is said that the theory and practice of British art are subject to the influence of the British school-girl, and that he is unworthy the name of artist whose achievement is of a kind to call a blush to the cheek of youth. Byron was contemptuous of youth, and did not hesitate to write—in *Beppo* and in *Cain*, in *Manfred* and *Don Juan* and the *Vision*—exactly as he pleased. In three words, he made himself offensively conspicuous, and from being infinitely popular became utterly contemptible. Too long had people listened to the scream of this eagle in wonder and in perturbation, and the moment he disappeared they grew ashamed of their emotion and angry with its cause, and began to hearken to other and more melodious voices—to Shelley and Keats, to Wordsworth and Coleridge and the 'faultless and fervent melodies of Tennyson.' In course of time Byron was forgotten, or only remembered with disdain; and when Thackeray, the representative Briton, the artist Philistine, the foe of all that is excessive or abnormal or rebellious, took it upon himself to flout the author of *Don Juan* openly and to lift up his heavy hand against the fops and fanatics who had affected the master's humours, he did so amid general applause. Meanwhile, however, the genius and the personality of Byron had come to be vital influences all the world over, and his voice had been recognised as the most human and the least insular raised on English ground since Shakespeare's. In Russia he had created Pushkin and Lermontoff; in Germany he had awakened Heine, inspired Schumann, and been saluted as an equal by the poet of *Faust* himself; in Spain he had had a share in moulding the noisy and unequal talent of Espronceda; in Italy he had helped to develop and to shape the melancholy and daring genius of Leopardi; and in France he had been one of the presiding forces of a great æsthetic revolution. To the men of 1830 he was a special and peculiar hero. Hugo turned in his wake to Spain and Italy and the East for inspiration. Musset, as Mr. Swinburne has said—too bitterly and strongly said— became in a fashion a Kaled to his Lara, 'his female page or attendant dwarf.' He was in some sort the grandsire of the Buridan and the Antony of Dumas. Berlioz went to him for the material for his *Harold en Italie*, his *Corsaire* overture, and his *Episode*. Delacroix painted the *Barque de Don Juan* from him, with the *Massacre de Scio*, the *Marino Faliero*, the

Combat du Giaour et du Pacha, and many a notable picture more. Is it at all surprising that M. Taine should have found heart to say that alone among modern poets Byron 'atteint à la cime'? or that Mazzini should have reproached us with our unaccountable neglect of him and with our scandalous forgetfulness of the immense work done by him in giving a 'European *rôle* . . . to English literature' and in awakening all over the Continent so much 'appreciation and sympathy for England'?

Byron and Wordsworth.

He had his share in the work of making Matthew Arnold possible, but he is the antipodes of those men of culture and contemplation—those artists pensive and curious and sedately self-contained—whom Arnold best loved and of whom the nearest to hand is Wordsworth. Byron and Wordsworth are like the Lucifer and the Michael of the *Vision of Judgment*. Byron's was the genius of revolt, as Wordsworth's was the genius of dignified and useful submission; Byron preached the dogma of private revolution, Wordsworth the dogma of private apotheosis; Byron's theory of life was one of liberty and self-sacrifice, Wordsworth's one of self-restraint and self-improvement; Byron's practice was dictated by a vigorous and voluptuous egoism, Wordsworth's by a benign and lofty selfishness; Byron was the 'passionate and dauntless soldier of a forlorn hope,' Wordsworth a kind of inspired clergyman. Both were influences for good, and both are likely to be influences for good for some time to come. Which is the better and stronger is a question that can hardly be determined now. It is certain that Byron's star has waned, and that Wordsworth's has waxed; but it is also certain that there are moments in life when the *Ode to Venice* is almost as refreshing and as precious as the ode on the *Intimations*, and when the epic mockery of *Don Juan* is to the full as beneficial as the chaste philosophy of *The Excursion* and the *Ode to Duty*. Arnold was of course with Michael heart and soul, and was only interested in our Lucifer. He approached his subject in a spirit of undue deprecation. He thought it necessary to cite Scherer's opinion that Byron is but a coxcomb and a rhetorician: partly, it would appear, for the pleasure of seeming to agree with it in a kind of way and partly to have the satisfaction of distinguishing and of showing it to be a mistake. Then, he could not quote Goethe without apologising for the warmth of that consummate artist's expressions and explaining some of them away. Again, he was pitiful or disdainful, or both, of Scott's estimate; and he did not care to discuss the sentiment which made that great and good man think *Cain* and the *Giaour* fit stuff for family reading on a Sunday after prayers, though as Mr. Ruskin has pointed out, in one of the wisest and subtlest bits of criticism I know, the sentiment is both natural and beautiful, and should assist us not a little in the task of judging Byron and of knowing him for what he was. That Arnold should institute a comparison between Leopardi and Byron was probably inevitable: Leopardi had culture and the philosophic mind, which Byron had not; he is incapable of influencing the general heart, as Byron can; he is a critics' poet, which Byron can never be; he was always an artist, which Byron was not; and—it were Arnoldian to take the comparison seriously. Byron was not interested in words and phrases but in the greater truths of destiny and emotion. His empire is over the imagination and the passions. His personality was many-sided enough to make his egoism representative. And as mankind is wont to feel first and to think afterwards, a single one of his heart-cries may prove to the world of greater value as a moral agency than all the intellectual reflections that Leopardi contrived to utter. After examining this and that opinion and doubting over and deprecating them all, Arnold touched firm ground at last in a dictum of Mr. Swinburne's, the most pertinent and profound since those of Goethe, to the effect that in Byron there is a 'splendid and imperishable excellence which covers all his offences and outweighs all his defects: the excellence of sincerity and strength.' With this 'noble praise' our critic agreed so vigorously that it became the key-note of the latter part of his summing up, and in the end you found him declaring Byron the equal of Wordsworth, and asserting of this 'glorious pair' that 'when the year 1900 is turned, and the nation comes to recount her poetic glories in the century which has just then ended, the first names with her will be these.' The prophecy is as little like to commend itself to the pious votary of Keats as to the ardent Shelleyite: there are familiars of the Tennysonian Muse, the Sibyl of *Rizpah* and *Vastness* and *Lucretius* and *The Voyage*, to whom it must seem impertinent beyond the prophet's wont; there are—(but *they* scarce count)—who grub (as for truffles) for meanings in Browning. But it was not uttered to please, and in truth it has enough of plausibility to infuriate whatever poet-sects there be. Especially the Wordsworthians.

HUGO

His Critics.

To many Hugo was of the race of Æschylus and Shakespeare, a world-poet in the sense that Dante was, an artist supreme alike in genius and in accomplishment. To others he was but a great master of words and cadences, with a gift of lyric utterance and inspiration rarely surpassed but with a personality so vigorous and excessive as to reduce its literary expression—in epic, drama, fiction, satire and ode and song—to the level of work essentially subjective, in sentiment as in form, in intention as in effect. The debate is one in which the only possible arbiter is Time; and to Time the final judgment may be committed. What is certain is that there is one point on which both dissidents and devout—the heretics who deny with Matthew Arnold and the orthodox who worship with Mr. Swinburne and M. de Banville—are absolutely agreed. Plainly Hugo was the greatest man of letters of his day. It has been given to few or none to live a life so full of effort and achievement, so rich in honour and success and fame. Born almost with the century, he was a writer at fifteen, and at his death he was writing still; so that the record of his career embraces a period of more than sixty years. There is hardly a department of art to a foremost place in which he did not prove his right. From first to last; from the time of Chateaubriand to the time of Zola, he was a leader of men; and with his departure from the scene the undivided sovereignty of literature became a thing of the past like Alexander's empire.

Some Causes and Effects.

In 1826, in a second set of *Odes et Ballades*, he announced his vocation in unmistakeable terms. He was a lyric poet and the captain of a new emprise. His genius was too large and energetic to move at ease in the narrow garment prescribed as the poet's wear by the dullards and the pedants who had followed Boileau. He began to repeat the rhythms of Ronsard and the Pleiad; to deal in the richest rhymes and in words and verses tricked with new-spangled ore; to be curious in cadences, careless of stereotyped rules, prodigal of invention and experiment, defiant of much long recognised as good sense, contemptuous of much till then applauded as good taste. In a word, he was the Hugo of the hundred volumes we know: an artist, that is, endowed with a technical imagination of the highest quality, the very genius of style, and a sense of the plastic quality of words unequalled, perhaps, since Milton. The time was ripe for him: within France and without it was big with revolution. In verse there were the examples of André Chenier and

Lamartine; in prose the work of Rousseau and Diderot, of Bernardin de Saint-Pierre and Chateaubriand; in war and politics the tremendous tradition of Napoleon. Goethe and Schiller had recreated romance and established the foundations of a new palace of art; their theory and practice had been popularised in the novels of Walter Scott; and in the life and work of Byron the race had such an example of revolt, such an incitement to liberty and change, such a passionate and persuasive argument against authority and convention, as had never before been felt in art. Hugo like all great artists was essentially a child of his age: 'Rebellion lay in his way, and he found it.' In 1827 he published his *Cromwell*, and came forth as a rebel confessed and unashamed. It is an unapproachable production, tedious in the closet, impossible upon the stage; and to compare it to such work as that which at some and twenty Keats had given to the world—*Hyperion*, for instance, or the *Eve of St. Agnes*—is to glory in the name of Briton. But it had its value then, and as an historical document it has its value now. The preface was at once a profession of faith and a proclamation of war. It is crude, it is limited, it is mistaken, in places it is even absurd. But from the moment of its appearance the old order was practically closed. It prepared the way for *Albertus* and for *Antony*, for *Rolla* and the *Tour de Nesle*; and it was also the '*fiat lux*' in deference to which the world has accepted with more or less of resignation the partial eclipse of art and morals effected in *Salammbô* and *l'Education sentimentale* and the Egyptian darkness achieved in work like *la Terre* and *une Vie* and *les Blasphèmes*. In its ringing periods, its plangent antitheses and æsthetic epigrams, it preluded and vindicated the excesses of whatsoever manifestations of romanticism mankind and the arts have since been called upon to consider and endure: from the humours of Petrus Borel to the experiments of Claude Monet and the 'discoveries' of Richard Wagner.

Environment.

It is too often forgotten that from the first Hugo was associated with men of pretensions and capacities not greatly inferior to his own, and that in no direction was victory the work of his single arm. In painting the initiative had been taken years before the publication of the *Cromwell* manifesto by Géricault with the famous *Radeau de la Méduse*, and by Delacroix with the *Dante et Virgile* (1822) and the *Massacre de Scio* (1823). In music Berlioz, at this time a student in the Conservatoire, was fighting hard against Cherubini and the bewigged ones for liberty of expression and leave to admire and imitate the audacities of Weber and Beethoven, and three years hence, in the year of *Hernani*, was to set his mark upon the art with the *Symphonie fantastique*. On the stage as early as 1824 Frédérick and Firmin had realised in the personages of Macaire and Bertrand the grotesque ideal, the combination of humour and terror, of which the character of Cromwell was put forward as the earliest expression, and had realised it so completely that their work has taken rank with the greater and the more lasting results of the movement. In the literature of drama the old order was ruined and the victory won on all essential points not in 1830 with *Hernani* but in 1829 with *Henri Trois et sa Cour*, the first of the innumerable successes of Alexandre Dumas, who determined at a single stroke the fundamental qualities of structure and form and material, and left his chief no question to solve save that of diction and style. Musset's earlier poems date from 1828, the year of *les Orientales*, Gautier's from 1830; and these are also the dates of Balzac's *Chouans* and *la Peau de Chagrin*. Moreover, among the intimates of the young leader were men like Sainte-Beuve, who was two years his junior, and the brothers Deschamps: whose influence was doubtless exerted more frequently to encourage than to repress. Towards the end we lost sight of all this, and saw in Victor Hugo not so much the most glorious survival of romanticism as romanticism itself, the movement in flesh and blood, the revolution in general 'summed up and closed' in a single figure. This agreeable view of things was Hugo's own. From the beginning he took himself with perfect seriousness, and his followers, however enthusiastic in admiration, had excellent warrant from above. 'Il *trône trop*,' says Berlioz of him somewhere; and M. Maxime du

Camp has given an edifying account of the means he was wont to use to make himself beloved and honoured by the youth who came to him for counsel and encouragement. How perfectly he succeeded in this the political part of his function is matter of history. Gautier's first visit to him was that of a devotee to his divinity; and years afterwards the good poet confessed that not even in pitch darkness and in a cellar fathoms under ground should he dare to whisper to himself that a verse of the Master's was bad. So far as devotion went there were innumerable Gautiers. Sainte-Beuve was not long a pillar of orthodoxy; Dumas was always conscious of his own pre-eminence in certain qualities, and made light of Hugo's dramas as candidly as he made much of the style in which they are written; and when some creature of unwisdom saluted Delacroix as 'the Hugo of painting,' the artist of the *Marino Faliero* and the *Barque de Don Juan* resented the compliment with bitterness. But these were exceptions. The youth of 1830 were Hugolaters almost to a man.

Equipment and Achievement.

Their enthusiasm was not all irrational. Hugo's supremacy was not that he was the greatest artist in essentials, for here Dumas was immeasurably his superior. It was not that he knew best the heart of man, or had apprehended most thoroughly the conditions of life; for Balzac so far surpassed him in these sciences that comparison was impossible. It was not that he sang the truest song or uttered the deepest word, for Musset is the poet of *Rolla* and the *Nuits* in verse and the poet of *Fantasio* and *Lorenzaccio* and *Carmosine* in prose. But the epoch Hugo represented was interested in the manner rather than the substance of things: the revolution at whose front he had been set and whose most shining figure he became was largely a revolution of externals. With an immense amount of enthusiasm there was, as Sainte-Beuve confessed, an incredible amount of ignorance—so that *Cromwell* was supposed to be historical; and with a passionate delight in form there co-existed a strangely imperfect understanding of material—so that *Hernani* was supposed to be Shakespearean. To this ignorance and to this imperfect understanding Hugo owed a certain part of his authority; the other and greater he got from his unrivalled mastery of style, from his extraordinary skill as an artist in words. To the opposing faction his innovations were horrible: his verse was poison, his example an outrage, his prosody a violation of all laws, his rhymes and tropes and metaphors so many offences against Heaven and the Muse. But to the ardent youngsters who fought beneath his banner it was his to give a something priceless and unique—a something glorious to France and never before exampled in her literature. For the distichs of Boileau—'strong, heavy, useful, like pairs of tongs,'—he found them alexandrines with the leap and sparkle of sea waves and the sound of clashing swords and the colours of sunset and the dawn. They were tired of whitewash and cold distemper; and he gave them hangings of brocade and tapestries of price and tissues stiff with gold and glowing with new dyes. He flung them handfuls of jewels where his rivals scattered handfuls of marbles. And they paid him for his gifts with an intemperance of worship, a fury of belief, a rapture of admiration, such as no other man has known. The substance was striking, was peculiar, was novel and full of charm; but the manner was all this and something besides—was magnificent, was intoxicating, was irresistible; and Victor Hugo by virtue of it became the foremost man of literary France. The great battle of *Hernani* was merely a battle of style. From Dumas the artist of *Henri Trois* and *Antony*, the language of Boileau was safe enough; and his triumph, all-important and significant as it was, seemed neither fatal nor abominable. It was another matter with *Hernani*. Its success meant ruin for the Academy and destruction for the idiom of Delille and M. de Jouy; and the classicists mustered in force, and did their utmost to stay the coming wrath and arrest the impending doom. They failed of course; for they fought with a vague yet limited apprehension of the question at issue, they had nothing to give in place of the thing they hated. And Victor Hugo was made captain of the victorious host, while the men who might have been in a certain sort his rivals took service as lieutenants, and accepted his ensign for their own.

His Diary.

All his life long he was addicted to attitude; all his life long he was a *poseur* of the purest water. He seems to have considered the affectation of superiority an essential quality in art; for just as the cock in Mrs. Poyser's apothegm believed that the sun got up to hear him crow, so to the poet of the *Légende* and the *Contemplations* it must have seemed as if the human race existed but to consider the use he made of his 'oracular tongue.' How tremendous his utterances sometimes were—informed with what majesty yet with what brilliance—is one of the things that every schoolboy knows. One no more needs to insist upon the merits of his best manner than to emphasise the faults of his worst. At his best as at his worst, however, he was always an artist in his way. His speech was nothing if not artificial—in the good sense of the word sometimes and sometimes in the bad. Simplicity (it seemed) was impossible to him. In the quest of expression, the cult of antithesis, the pursuit of effect, he sacrificed directness and plainness with not less consistency than complacency. In that tissue of 'apocalyptic epigram' which to him was style there was no room for truth and soberness. His Patmos was a place of mirrors, and before them he draped himself in his phrases like Frederick in the mantle of Ruy Blas. That this grandiosity was unnatural and unreal was proved by the publication of *Choses Vues*. When Hugo wrote for himself he wrote almost as simply and straightforwardly as Dumas. The effect is disconcerting. You rub your eyes in amazement. It is evidently Hugo. But Hugo plain, sober, direct? Hugo without rhetoric? Hugo declining antithesis and content to be no gaudier than his neighbours? Hugo expressing himself in the fearless old fashion of pre-romantic ages? A page of commonplace from Mr. Meredith, a book for boarding-schools by M. Zola, were not more startling.

For and Against.

Some primary qualities of his genius are pretty evenly balanced by some primary faults. Thus, for breadth and brilliance of conception, for energy and sweep of imagination, for the power of dealing as a master with the greater forces of nature, he is unsurpassed among modern men. But the conception is too often found to be empty as well as spacious; the imagination is too often tainted with insincerity; in his dramas of the elements there are too many such falsehoods as abound in his dramas of the emotions. Again, he is sometimes grand and often grandiose; but he has a trick of affecting the grandiose and the grand which is constant and intolerable. He had the genius of style in such fulness as entitles him to rank with the great artists in words of all time. His sense of verbal colour and verbal music is beyond criticism; his rhythmical capacity is something prodigious. He so revived and renewed the language of France that in his hands it became an instrument not unworthy to compete with Shakespeare's English and the German of Goethe and Heine; and in the structure and capacity of all manner of French metrical forms he effected such a change that he may fairly be said to have received the orchestra of Rameau from his predecessors and to have bequeathed his heirs the orchestra of Berlioz. On the other hand; in much of his later work his mannerisms in prose and in verse are discomfortably glaring; the outcome of his unsurpassable literary faculty is often no more than a parade or triumph of the vocables; there were times when his brain appears to have become a mere machine for the production of antitheses and sterile conceits. What is perhaps more damning than all, his work is saturate in his own remarkable personality, and is objective only here and there. His dramas are but five-act lyrics, his epics the romance of an egoist, his history is confession, his criticism the opinions of Victor Hugo. Even his lyrics, the 'fine flower' of his genius, the loveliest expression of the language, have not escaped reproach as a 'Psalter of Subjectivity.' Even his essays in prose romance—a form of art on which he has stamped his image and superscription in a manner all his own, the work by which he is best known to humanity at large—are vitiated by the same defect. For one that believes in Bishop Myriel as Bishop Myriel there are a hundred who see in him only a pose of Victor Hugo; it is the same with Ursel and Javert, with Cimourdain and Lantenac and Josiane; the very *pieuvre* of *les Travailleurs* is a Hugolater at heart. It is a proof of his commanding personality, that in spite of these objections he held in enchantment the hearts and minds of men for over sixty years. He is almost a literature in himself; and if it be true that his work is as wholly lacking in the radiant sanity of Shakespeare's as it is in the exquisite good sense of Voltaire's, it is also true that he left the world far richer than he found it.

What Lives of Him.

To select an anthology from his work were surely the pleasantest of tasks. One richer in grace and passion and sweetness might he chosen out of Musset; one wrought more truly of the finer stuff of humanity as well as more bountifully touched with tact and dignity and temper from the work of Tennyson. But the Hugo selection would combine the rarest technical merits with a set of interests all its own. It would give, for instance, the *Stella* of the *Châtiments* and the *Pauvres Gens* of the *Légende*. On one page would be found that admirable *Souvenir de la Nuit du Quatre*, which is at once the impeachment and the condemnation of the Coup d'État; and on another the little epic of *Eviradnus*, with its immortal serenade, a culmination of youth and romance and love:

> 'Si tu veux, faisons un rêve.
> Montons sur deux palefrois.
> Tu m'emmènes, je t'enlève.
> L'oiseau chante dans les bois.
>
> . . . . .
>
> Allons-nous-en par l'Autriche!
> Nous aurons l'aube à nos fronts.
> Je serai grand et toi riche,
> Puisque nous nous aimerons.
>
> . . . . .
>
> Tu seras dame et moi comte.
> Viens, mon œeur s'épanouit.
> Viens, nous conterons ce conte
> Aux étoiles de la nuit.'

Here, a summary of all the interests of romanticism, would be the complaint of Gastibelza:

'Un jour d'été, où tout était lumière,
  Vie et douceur,
Elle s'en vint jouer dans la rivière
  Avec sa sœur.
Je vis le pied de sa jeune compagne
  Et son genou . . .—
Le vent qui vient à travers la montagne
  Me rendra fou!'—

here the adorable *Vieille Chanson du Jeune Temps*:

'Rose, droite sur ses hanches,
Leva son beau bras tremblant
Pour prendre une mûre aux branches:
Je ne vis pas son bras blanc.

Une eau courait, fraîche et creuse,
Sur les mousses de velours;
Et la nature amoureuse
Dormait dans les grands bois sourds.'—

and here, not unworthy to be remembered with *Proud Maisie*, that wonderful harmony of legend and superstition and the facts and dreams of common life, the death-song of Fantine:

'Nous acheterons de bien belles choses,
  En nous promenant le long de faubourgs.

La Vierge-Marie auprès de mon poêle
  Est venue hier, en manteau brodé,
Et m'a dit: Voici, caché sous mon voile,
  Le petit qu'un jour tu m'as demandé.
Courez à la ville; ayez de la toile,
  Achetez du fil, achetez un dé.

Les bluets sont bleus, les roses sont roses,
  Les bluets sont bleus, j'aime mes amours.'

And from this masterpiece of simple and direct emotion, which to me has always seemed the high-water mark of Hugo's lyrical achievement as well as the most human of his utterances, one might pass on to masterpieces of another inspiration: to the luxurious and charming graces of *Sara la Baigneuse*; to the superb crescendo and diminuendo of *les Djinns*; to 'Si vous n'avez rien à me dire,' that daintiest of songlets; to the ringing rhymes and gallant spirit of the *Pas d'Armes du Roi Jean*:

'Sus, ma bête,
De façon
Que je fête

Ce grison!
Je te baille
Pour ripaille
Plus de paille,
Plus de son,

Qu'un gros frère,
Gai, friand,
Ne peut faire,
Mendiant
Par les places
Où tu passes,
De grimaces
En priant!'—

to the melodious tenderness of 'Si tu voulais, Madelaine';
to the gay music of the *Stances à Jeanne*:

'Je ne me mets pas en peine
Du clocher ni du beffroi.
Je ne sais rien de la reine,
Et je ne sais rien du roi.'—

to the admirable song of the wind of the sea:

'Quels sont les bruits sourds?
Ecoutez vers l'onde
Cette voix profonde
Qui pleure toujours,
Et qui toujours gronde,

Quoiqu'un son plus claire
Parfois l'interrompe . . .
Le vent de la mer
Souffle dans sa trompe.'—

to the *Romance Mauresque*, to the barbaric fury of *les Reîtres*, to the magnificent rodomontade of the *Romancero du Cid*. 'J'en passe, et des meilleurs,' as Ruy Gomez observes of his ancestors. Here at any rate are jewels enough to furnish forth a casket that should be one of the richest of its kind! The worst is, they are most of them not necessaries but luxuries. It is impossible to conceive of life without Shakespeare and Burns, without *Paradise Lost* and the *Intimations* ode and the immortal pageant of the *Canterbury Tales*; but (the technical question apart) to imagine it wanting Hugo's lyrics is easy enough. The largesse of which he was so prodigal has but an arbitrary and conventional value. Like the magician's money much has changed, almost in the act of distribution, into withered leaves; and such of it as seems minted of good metal is not for general circulation.

HEINE

The Villainy Translation.

 Heine had a light hand with the branding-iron, and marked his subjects not more neatly than indelibly. And really he alone were capable of dealing adequate vengeance upon his translators. His verse has only violent lovers or violent foes; indifference is impossible. Once read as it deserves, it becomes one of the loveliest of our spiritual acquisitions. We hate to see it tampered with; we are on thorns as the translator approaches, and we resent his operations as an individual hurt, a personal affront. What business has he to be trampling among our borders and crushing our flowers with his stupid hobnails? Why cannot he carry his zeal for topsy-turvy horticulture elsewhere? He comes and lays a brutal hand on our pet growths, snips off their graces, shapes them anew according to his own ridiculous ideal, paints and varnishes them with a villainous compound of his contrivance, and then bids us admire the effect and thank him for its production! Is any name too hard for such a creature? and could any vengeance be too deadly? If he walked into your garden and amused himself so with your cabbages, you could put him in prison. But into your poets he can stump his way at will, and upon them he can do his pleasure. And he does it. How many men have brutalised the elegance, the grace, the winning urbanity of Horace! By how many coarse and stupid fingers has Catullus been smudged and fumbled and mauled! To turn *Faust* into English (in the original metres) is a fashionable occupation; there are more perversions of the *Commedia* than one cares to recall; there is scarce a great or even a good work of the human mind but has been thus bedevilled and deformed. *Don Quixote, le Père Goriot, The Frogs, The Decameron*—the trail of the translator is over them all. Messrs. Payne and Lang and Swinburne have turned poor Villon into a citizen of Bedford Park, Fitzgerald and Florence Macarthy have Englished Calderon, Messrs. Pope, Gladstone and others have done their worst with Homer. If Rossetti had not succeeded with *la Vita Nuova*, if Fitzgerald had not ennobled Omar, if Mr. Lang had not bettered upon Banville and Gérard de Nerval, the word 'translator' would be odious as the word 'occupy.' And 'occupy' on the authority of Mrs. Dorothy Tearsheet is an odious word indeed.

The Proof of It.

The fact is, the translator too often forgets the difference between his subject and himself; he is too often a common graveyard mason that would play the sculptor. And it is not nearly enough for him to be a decent craftsman. To give an adequate idea of an artist's work a man must be himself an artist of equal force and versatility with his original. The typical translator makes clever enough verses, but Heine's accomplishment is remote from him as Heine's genius. He perverts his author as rhyme and rhythm will. No charge of verbal inaccuracy need therefore be made, for we do not expect a literal fidelity in our workman. Let him convey the spirit of his original, and that, so far as meaning goes, is enough. But we do expect of him a something that shall recall his author's form, his author's personality, his author's charm of diction and of style; and here it is that such an interpreter as Sir Theodore Martin (say) fails with such assurance and ill-fortune. The movement of Heine's rhythms, simple as they seem, is not spontaneous; it is an effect of art: the poet laboured at his cadences as at his meanings. Artificial he is, but he has the wonderful quality of never seeming artificial. His verses dance and sway like the nixies he loved. Their every motion seems informed with the perfect suavity and spontaneity of pure nature. They tinkle down the air like sunset bells, they float like clouds, they wave like flowers, they twitter like skylarks, they have in them something of the swiftness and the certainty of exquisite physical sensations. In such a transcript as Sir Theodore's all this is lost: Heine becomes a mere prentice-metrist; he sets the teeth on edge as surely as Browning himself; the verse that recalled a dance of naiads suggests a springless cart on a Highland road;

Terpsichore is made to prance a hobnailed breakdown. The poem disappears, and in its place you have an indifferent copy of verses. You look at the pages from afar, and your impression is that they are not unlike Heine; you look into them, and Heine has vanished. The man is gone, and only an awkward, angular, clumsily articulated, entirely preposterous lay-figure remains to show that the translator has been by.

MATTHEW ARNOLD

His Verse.

In every page of Arnold the poet there is something to return upon and to admire. There are faults, and these of a kind this present age is ill-disposed to condone. The rhymes are sometimes poor; the movement of the verse is sometimes uncertain and sometimes slow; the rhythms are obviously simple always; now and then the intention and effect are cold even to austerity, are bald to uncomeliness. But then, how many of the rarer qualities of art and inspiration are represented here, and here alone in modern work! There is little of that delight in material for material's sake which is held to be essential to the composition of a great artist; there is none of that rapture of sound and motion and none of that efflorescence of expression which are deemed inseparable from the endowment of the true singer. For any of those excesses in technical accomplishment, those ecstasies in the use of words, those effects of sound which are so rich and strange as to impress the hearer with something of their author's own emotion of creation—for any, indeed, of the characteristic attributes of modern poetry—you shall turn to him in vain. In matters of form this poet is no romantic but a classic to the marrow. He adores his

Shakespeare, but he will none of his Shakespeare's fashions. For him the essentials are dignity of thought and sentiment and distinction of manner and utterance. It is no aim of his to talk for talking's sake, to express what is but half felt and half understood, to embody vague emotions and nebulous fancies in language no amount of richness can redeem from the reproach of being nebulous and vague. In his scheme of art there is no place for excess, however magnificent and Shakespearean—for exuberance, however overpowering and Hugoesque. Human and interesting in themselves, the ideas apparelled in his verse are completely apprehended; natural in themselves, the experiences he pictures are intimately felt and thoroughly perceived. They have been resolved into their elements by the operation of an almost Sophoclean faculty of selection, and the effect of their presentation is akin to that of a gallery of Greek marbles.

His Failure.

Other poets say anything—say everything that is in them. Browning lived to realise the myth of the Inexhaustible Bottle; Mr. William Morris is nothing: if not fluent and copious; Mr. Swinburne has a facility that would seem impossible if it were not a living fact; even the Laureate is sometimes prodigal of unimportant details, of touches insignificant and superfluous, of words for words' sake, of cadences that have no reason of being save themselves. Matthew Arnold alone says only what is worth saying. In other words, he selects: from his matter whatever is impertinent is eliminated and only what is vital is permitted to remain. Sometimes he goes a little astray, and his application of the principle on which Sophocles and Homer wrought results in failure. But in these instances it will always be found, I think, that the effect is due not to the principle nor the poet's application of it but to the poet himself, who has exceeded his commission, and attempted more than is in him to accomplish. The case is rare with Arnold, one of whose qualities—and by no means the least Hellenic of them—was a fine consciousness of his limitations. But that he failed, and failed considerably, it were idle to deny. There is *Merope* to bear witness to the fact; and of *Merope* what is there to say? Evidently it is an imitation Greek play: an essay, that is, in a form which ceased long since to have any active life, so that the attempt to revive it—to create a soul under the ribs of very musty death—is a blunder alike in sentiment and in art. As evidently Arnold is no dramatist. Empedocles, the Strayed Reveller, even the Forsaken Merman, all these are expressions of purely personal feeling—are so many metamorphoses of Arnold. In *Merope* there is no such basis of reality. The poet was never on a level with his argument. He knew little or nothing of his characters—of Merope or Æpytus or Polyphontes, of Arcas or Laias or even the Messenger; at every step the ground is seen shifting under his feet; he is comparatively void of matter, and his application of the famous principle is labour lost. He is winnowing the wind; he is washing not gold but water.

His Triumphs.

It is other-guess work with *Empedocles*, the *Dejaneira* fragment, *Sohrab and Rustum*, the *Philomela*, his better work in general, above all with the unique and unapproached *Balder Dead*. To me this last stands alone in modern art for simple majesty of conception, sober directness and potency of expression, sustained dignity of thought and sentiment and style, the complete presentation of whatever is essential, the stern avoidance of whatever is merely decorative: indeed for every Homeric quality save rhythmical vitality and rapidity of movement. Here, for example, is something of that choice yet ample suggestiveness—the only true realism because the only perfect ideal of realisation—for which the similitudes of the 'Ionian father of his race' are pre-eminently distinguished:—

> 'And as a spray of honeysuckle flowers
> Brushes across a tired traveller's face
> Who shuffles through the deep dew-moistened dust
> On a May evening, in the darken'd lanes,

And starts him, that he thinks a ghost went by—
So Hoder brushed by Hermod's side.'

Here is Homer's direct and moving because most human and comprehensive touch in narrative:—

'But from the hill of Lidskialf Odin rose,
The throne, from which his eye surveys the world;
And mounted Sleipner, and in darkness rode
To Asgard. And the stars came out in heaven,
High over Asgard, to light home the king.
But fiercely Odin gallop'd, moved in heart;
And swift to Asgard, to the gate, he came.
And terribly the hoofs of Sleipner rang
Along the flinty floor of Asgard streets,
And the Gods trembled on their golden beds
Hearing the wrathful Father coming home—
For dread, for like a whirlwind Odin came.
And to Valhalla's gate he rode, and left
Sleipner; and Sleipner went to his own stall;
And in Valhalla Odin laid him down.'

And here—to have done with evidence of what is known to every one—here is the Homeric mariner, large and majestic and impersonal, of recording speech:—

'Bethink ye, Gods, is there no other way?—
Speak, were not this a way, a way for Gods?
If I, if Odin, clad in radiant arms,
Mounted on Sleipner, with the warrior Thor
Drawn in his car beside me, and my sons,
All the strong brood of Heaven, to swell my train,
Should make irruption into Hela's realm,
And set the fields of gloom ablaze with light,
And bring in triumph Balder back to Heaven?'

One has but to contrast such living work as this with the 'mouldering realm' of *Merope* to feel the difference with a sense of pain;

'For doleful are the ghosts, the troops of dead,
Whom Hela with austere control presides';

while this in its plain, heroic completeness is touched with a stately life that is a presage of immortality. It is evident, indeed, that Arnold wrote *Balder Dead* in his most fortunate hour, and that *Merope* is his one serious mistake in literature. For a genius thus peculiar and introspective drama—the presentation of character through action—is impossible; to a method thus reticent and severe drama—the expression of emotion in action—is improper. 'Not here, O Apollo!' It is written that none shall bind his brows with the twin laurels of epos and drama. Shakespeare did not, nor could Homer; and how should Matthew Arnold?

His Prose.

He has opinions and the courage of them; he has assurance and he has charm; he writes with an engaging clearness. It is very possible to disagree with him; but it is difficult indeed to resist his many graces of manner, and decline to be entertained and even interested by the variety and quality of his matter. He was described as 'the most un-English of Britons,' the most cosmopolitan of islanders; and you feel as you read him that in truth his mind was French. He took pattern by Goethe, and was impressed by Leopardi; he was judiciously classic, but his romanticism was neither hidebound nor inhuman; he apprehended Heine and Marcus Aurelius, Spinoza and Sainte-Beuve, Joubert and Maurice de Guérin, Wordsworth and Pascal, Rachel and Sarah Bernhardt, Burke and Arthur Clough, Eliza Cook and Homer; he was an authority on education, poetry, civilisation, the *Song of Roland,* the love-letters of Keats, the Genius of Bottles, the significance of *eutrapelos* and *eutrapelia*. In fact, we have every reason to be proud of him. For the present is a noisy and affected age; it is given overmuch to clamorous devotion and extravagant repudiation; there is an element of swagger in all its words and ways; it has a distressing and immoral turn for publicity. Matthew Arnold's function was to protest against its fashions by his own intellectual practice, and now and then to take it to task and to call it to order. He was not particularly original, but he had in an eminent degree the formative capacity, the genius of shaping and developing, which is a chief quality of the French mind and which is not so common among us English as our kindest critics would have us believe. He would take a handful of golden sentences—things wisely thought and finely said by persons having authority—and spin them into an exquisite prelection; so that his work with all the finish of art retains a something of the freshness of those elemental truths on which it was his humour to dilate. He was, that is to say, an artist in ethics as in speech, in culture as in ambition. 'Il est donné,' says Sainte-Beuve, 'de nos jours, à un bien petit nombre, même parmi les plus délicats et ceux qui les apprécient le mieux, de recueillir, d'ordonner sa vie selon ses admirations et selon ses goûts, avec suite, avec noblesse.' That is true enough; but Arnold was one of the few, and might 'se vanter d'être resté fidèle à soi-même, à son premier et à son plus beau passé.' He was always a man of culture in the good sense of the word; he had many interests in life and art, and his interests were sound and liberal; he was a good critic of both morals and measures, both of society and of literature, because he was commonly at the pains of understanding his matter before he began to speak about it. It is therefore not surprising that the part he played was one of considerable importance or that his influence was healthy in the main. He was neither prophet nor pedagogue but a critic pure and simple. Too well read to be violent, too nice in his discernment to be led astray beyond recovery in any quest after strange gods, he told the age its faults and suggested such remedies as the study of great men's work had suggested to him. If his effect was little that was not his fault. He returned to the charge with imperturbable good temper, and repeated his remarks—which are often exasperating in effect—with a mixture of mischievousness and charm, of superciliousness and sagacity, and a serene dexterity of phrase, unique in modern letters.

HOMER AND THEOCRITUS

The Odyssey.

I think that of all recent books the two that have pleased me best and longest are those delightful renderings into English prose of the Greek of Homer and Theocritus, which we owe, the one to Messrs. Henry Butcher and Andrew Lang and the other to Mr. Lang's unaided genius. To read this *Odyssey* of theirs is to have a breath of the clear, serene airs that blew through the antique Hellas; to catch a glimpse of the large, new morning light that bathes the seas and highlands of the young heroic world. In a space of shining and fragrant clarity you have a vision of marble columns and stately cities, of men august in single-heartedness and strength and women comely and simple and superb as goddesses; and with a music of leaves and winds and waters, of plunging ships and clanging armours, of girls at song and kindly gods discoursing, the sunny-eyed heroic age is revealed in all its nobleness, in all its majesty, its candour, and its charm. The air is yet plangent with echoes of the leaguer of Troy, and Odysseus the ready-at-need goes forth upon his wanderings: into the cave of Polypheme, into the land of giants, into the very regions of the dead: to hear among the olive trees the voice of Circe, the sweet witch, singing her magic song as she fares to and fro before her golden loom; to rest and pine in the islet of Calypso, the kind sea-goddess; to meet with Nausicaa, loveliest of mortal maids; to reach his Ithaca, and do battle with the Wooers, and age in peace and honour by the side of the wise Penelope. The day is yet afar when, as he sailed out to the sunset and the mysterious west,

> Sol con un legno, e con quella compagna
> Picciola, dalla qual non fue deserto,

the great wind rushed upon him from the new-discovered land, and so ended his journeyings for ever; and all with him is energy and tact and valour and resource, as becomes the captain of an indomitable human soul. His society is like old d'Artagnan's: it invigorates, renews, inspires. I had rather lack the friendship of the good Alonso Quijada himself than the brave example of these two.

The Idylls.

With certain differences it is the same with our Theocritus. From him, too, the mind is borne back to a 'happier age of gold,' when the world was younger than now, and men were not so weary nor so jaded nor so highly civilised as they choose to think themselves. Shepherds still piped, and maidens still listened to their piping. The old gods had not been discrowned and banished; and to fishers drawing their nets the coasts yet kept a something of the trace of amorous Polypheme, the rocks were peopled with memories of his plaint to Galatea. Inland, among the dim and thymy woods, bee-haunted and populous with dreams of dryad and oread, there were rumours of Pan; and dwellers under thatch—the goatherd mending his sandals, the hind carving his new staff, the girls who busked them for the vintaging—were conscious, as the wind went by among the beeches and the pines, and brought with it the sounds of a lonely and mysterious night, that hard by them in the starry darkness the divine Huntress was abroad, and about the base of Ætna she and her forest maids drove the chase with horn and hound. In the cities ladies sang the psalm of Adonis brought back from 'the stream eternal of Acheron.' Under the mystic moon love-lorn damsels did their magic rites, and knit up spells of power to bring home the men they loved. Among the vines and under the grey olives songs were singing of Daphnis all day long. There were junketings and dancings and harvest-homes for ever toward; the youths went by to the gymnasium, and the girls stood near to watch them as they went; the cicalas sang, the air was fragrant with apples and musical with the sound of flutes and running water; while the blue Sicilian sky laughed over all, and the soft Sicilian sea encircled the land and its lovers with a ring of sapphire and silver. To translate Theocritus, wrote Sainte-

Beuve, is as if one sought to carry away in one's hand a patch of snow that has lain forgotten through the summer in a cranny of the rocks of Ætna:—'On a fait trois pas à peine, que cette neige déjà est fondue. On est heureux s'il en reste assez du moins pour donner le vif sentiment de la fraîcheur.' But Mr. Lang has so rendered into English the graces of the loveliest of Dorian singers that he has earned the thanks of every lover of true literature. Every one should read his book, for it will bring him face to face with a very prince among poets and with a very summer among centuries. That Theocritus was a rare and beautiful master there is even in this English transcript an abundance of evidence. Melancholy apart, he was the Watteau of the old Greek world—an exquisite artist, a rare poet, a true and kindly soul; and it is very good to be with him. We have changed it all of course, and are as fortunate as we can expect. But it is good to be with Theocritus, for he lets you live awhile in the happy age and under the happy heaven that were his. He gives you leave and opportunity to listen to the tuneful strife of Lacon and Comatas; to witness the duel in song between Corydon and Battus; to talk of Galatea pelting with apples the barking dog of her love-lorn Polypheme; under the whispering elms, to lie drinking with Eucritus and Lycidas by the altar of Demeter, 'while she stands smiling by, with sheaves and poppies in her hand.'

Old Lamps and New.

It is relief unspeakable to turn from the dust and din and chatter of modern life, with its growing trade in heroes and its poverty of men, its innumerable regrets and ambitions and desires, to this immense tranquillity, this candid and shining calm. They had no Irish Question then, you can reflect, nor was theology invented. Men were not afraid of life nor ashamed of death; and you could be heroic without a dread of clever editors, and hospitable without fear of rogues, and dutiful for no hope of illuminated scrolls. Odysseus disguised as Irus is still Odysseus and august. How comes it that Mr. Gladstone in rags and singing ballads would be only fit for a police-station? that Lord Salisbury hawking cocoa-nuts would instantly suggest the purlieus of Petticoat Lane? Is the fault in ourselves? Can it be that we have deteriorated so much as that? Nerves, nerves, nerves! . . . These many centuries the world has had neuralgia; and what has come of it is that Robert Elsmere is an ideal, and the bleat of the sentimentalist might almost be mistaken for the voice of living England.

RABELAIS

His Essence.

Rabelais is not precisely a book for bachelors and maids—at times, indeed, is not a book for grown men. There are passages not to be read without a blush and a sensation of sickness: the young giant which is the Renaissance being filthy and gross as Nature herself at her grossest and her most filthy. It is argued that this is all deliberate—is an effect of premeditation: that Rabelais had certain home-truths to deliver to his generation, and delivered them in such terms as kept him from the fagot and the rope by bedaubing him with the renown of a common buffoon. But the argument is none of the soundest in itself, and may fairly be set aside as a piece of desperate special pleading, the work of counsel at their wits' end for matter of defence. For Rabelais clean is not Rabelais at all. His grossness is an essential component in his mental fabric, an element in whose absence he would be not Rabelais but somebody else. It inspires his practice of art to the full as thoroughly as it informs his theory of language. He not only employs it wherever it might be useful: he goes out of his way to find it, he shovels it in on any and every occasion, he bemerds his readers and himself with a gusto that assuredly is not a common characteristic of defensive operations. In him, indeed, the humour of Old France—the broad, rank, unsavoury *esprit gaulois*—found its heroic expression; he made use of it because he must; and we can no more eliminate it from his work than we can remove the quality of imagination from Shakespeare's or those of art and intellect from Ben Jonson's. Other men are as foul or fouler; but in none is foulness so inbred and so ingrained, from none is it so inseparable. Few have had so much genius, and in none else has genius been so curiously featured.

His Secret.

It is significant enough that with all this against him he should have been from the first a great moral and literary influence and the delight of the wisest and soundest minds the world has seen. Shakespeare read him, and Jonson; Montaigne, a greater than himself, is in some sort his descendant; Swift, in Coleridge's enlightening phrase, is 'anima Rabelaesii habitans in sicco'; to Sterne and Balzac and Molière he was a constant inspiration; unto this day his work is studied and his meanings are sought with almost religious devoutness; while his phrases have passed into the constitution of a dozen languages, and the great figures he scrawled across the face of the Renaissance have survived the movement that gave them being, and are ranked with the monuments of literature. Himself has given us the reasons in the prologue to the first book, where he tells of the likeness between Socrates and the boxes called Sileni, and discourses of the manifest resemblance of his own work with Socrates. 'Opening this box,' which is Socrates, says he, 'you would have found within it a heavenly and inestimable drug, a more than human understanding, an admirable virtue, matchless learning, invincible courage, inimitable sobriety, certain contentment of mind, perfect assurance, and an incredible disregard of all that for which men cunningly do so much watch, run, sail, fight, travel, toil, and turmoil themselves.' In such wise must his book be opened, and the 'high conceptions' with which it is stuffed will presently be apparent. Nay, more: you are to do with it even as a dog with a marrowbone. 'If you have seen him you might have remarked with what devotion and circumspection he watches and wards it; with what care he keeps it; how fervently he holds it; how prudently he gobbets it; with what affection he breaks it; with what diligence he sucks it.' And in the same way you 'by a sedulous lecture and frequent meditation' shall break the bone and suck out the marrow of these books. Since the advice was proffered, generation after generation of mighty wits have taken counsel with the Master, and his wisdom has through them been passed out into the practice of life, the evolution of society, the development of humanity. But the 'prince de toute sapience et de toute comédie' has not yet uttered his last word. He remains in the front of time as when he lived and wrote. The Abbey of Thelema and the education of Gargantua are still unrealised ideals; the Ringing Isle and the Isle of Papimany are in their essentials pretty much as he left them; Panurge, 'the pollarded man, the man with every faculty except the reason,' has bettered no whit for the three centuries of improvement that have passed since he was flashed into being. We—even we—have much to learn from Master Alcofribas, and until we have learned it well enough to put it into practice his work remains half done and his book still one to study.

SHAKESPEARE

A Parallel.

Shakespeare and Rembrandt have in common the faculty of quickening speculation and compelling the minds of men to combat and discussion. About the English poet a literature of contention has been in process of accretion ever since he was discovered to be Shakespeare; and about the Dutch painter and etcher there has gradually accumulated a literature precisely analogous in character and for the most part of equal quality. In such an age as this, when the creative faculty of the world is mainly occupied with commentary and criticism, the reason should not be far to seek. Both were giants; both were original and individual in the highest sense of the words; both were leagues ahead of their contemporaries, not merely as regards the matter of their message but also in respect of the terms of its delivery; each, moreover—and here one comes upon a capital point of contact and resemblance—each was at times prodigiously inferior to himself. Shakespeare often writes so ill that you hesitate to believe he could ever write supremely well; or, if this way of putting it seem indecorous and abominable, he very often writes so well that you are loth to believe he could ever have written thus extremely ill. There are passages in his work in which he reaches such heights of literary art as since his time no mortal has found accessible; and there are passages which few or none of us can read without a touch of that 'burning sense of shame' experienced in the presence of Mr. Poynter's *Diadumene* by the British Matron of *The Times* newspaper. Now, we have got to be so curious in ideals that we cannot away with the thought of imperfection. Our worship must have for its object something flawless, something utterly without spot or blemish. We can be satisfied with nothing less than an entire and perfect chrysolite; and we cannot taste our Shakespeare at his worst without experiencing not merely the burning sense of shame aforesaid but also a frenzy of longing to father his faults upon somebody else—Marlowe for instance, or Green, or Fletcher—and a fury of proving that our divinity was absolutely incapable of them. That Shakespeare varied—that the matchless prose and the not particularly lordly verse of *As You Like It* are by the same hand; that the master to whom we owe our Hamlet is also responsible for Gertrude and King Claudius; that he who gave us the agony of Lear and the ruin of Othello did likewise perpetrate the scene of Hector's murder, in manner so poor and in spirit so cynical and vile—is beyond all belief and patience; and we have argued the point to such an extent that we are all of us in Gotham, and a mooncalf like the ascription of whatever is good in Shakespeare to Lord Bacon is no prodigy but a natural birth.

SIDNEY

His Expression of Life.

Sidney's prime faults are affectation and conceit. His verses drip with fine love-honey; but it has been so clarified in meta-physics that much of its flavour and sweetness has escaped. Very often, too, the conceit embodied is preposterously poor. You have as it were a casket of finest gold elaborately wrought and embellished, and the gem within is a mere spangle of paste, a trumpery spikelet of crystal. No doubt there is a man's heart beating underneath; but so thick is the envelope of buckram and broidery and velvet through which it has to make itself audible that its pulsations are sometimes hard to count, while to follow it throb by throb is impossible. And if this be true of that *Astrophel and Stella* series in which the poet outpours the melodious heyday of his youth—in which he strives to embody a passion as rich and full as ever stirred man's blood—what shall be said of the *Arcadia*? In that 'cold pastoral' he is trying to give breath and substance to as thin and frigid a fashion as has ever afflicted literature; and though he put a great deal of himself into the result, still every one has not the true critical insight, and to most of us, I think, those glimpses of the lofty nature of the writer which make the thing written a thing of worth in the eyes of the few are merely invisible.

His Fame.

In thinking of Sidney, Ophelia's lament for Hamlet springs to the lips, and the heart reverts to that closing scene at Zutphen with a blessed sadness of admiration and regret. But frankly, is it not a fact that that fine last speech of his has more availed to secure him immortality than all his verse? They call him the English Bayard, and the Frenchman need not be displeasured by the comparison. But when you come to read his poetry you find that our Bayard had in him a strong dash of the pedant and a powerful leaven of the euphuist. Subtle, delicate, refined, with a keen and curious wit, a rare faculty of verse, a singular capacity of expression, an active but not always a true sense of form, he wrote for the few, and (it may be) the few will always love him. But his intellectual life, intense though it were, was lived among shadows and abstractions. He thought deeply, but he neither looked widely nor listened intently, and when all is said he remains no more than a brilliant amorist, too super-subtle for complete sincerity, whose fluency and sweetness have not improved with years.

TOURNEUR

His Style.

Tourneur was a fierce and bitter spirit. The words in which he unpacked his heart are vitalised with passion. He felt so keenly that oftentimes his phrase is the offspring of the emotion, so terse and vigorous and apt, so vivid and so potent and eager, it appears. As an instance of this avidity of wrath and scorn finding expression in words the fittest and most forcible, leaving the well-known scenes embalmed in Elia's praise, one might take the three or four single words in which Vindici (*The Revenger's Tragedy*), on as many several occasions, refers to the caresses of Spurio and the wanton Duchess. Each is of such amazing propriety, is so keenly discriminated, is so obviously the product of an imagination burning with rage and hate, that it strikes you like an affront: each is an incest taken in the fact and branded there and then. And this quality of verbal fitness, this power of so charging a phrase with energy and colour as to make it convey the emotion of the writer at the instant of inspiration, is perhaps the master quality of Tourneur's work.

His Matter.

They that would have it are many; they that achieve their desire are few. For in the minor artist the passionate—the elemental quality—is not often found: he being of his essence the ape or zany of his betters. Tourneur is not a great tragic. *The Atheist's Tragedy* is but grotesquely and extravagantly horrible; its personages are caricatures of passion; its comedy is inexpressibly sordid; its incidents are absurd when they are not simply abominable. But it is written in excellent dramatic verse and in a rich and brilliant diction, and it contains a number of pregnant epithets and ringing lines and violent phrases. And if you halve the blame and double the praise you will do something less than justice to that *Revenger's Tragedy* which is Tourneur's immortality. After all its companion is but a bastard of the loud, malignant, antic muse of Marston; the elegies are cold, elaborate, and very tedious; the *Transformed Metamorphosis* is better verse but harder reading than *Sordello* itself. But the *Revenger's Tragedy* has merit as a piece of art and therewith a rare interest as a window on the artist's mind. The effect is as of a volcanic landscape. An earthquake has passed, and among grisly shapes and blasted aspects here lurks and wanders the genius of ruin.

WALTON

The Compleat Angler.

I am told that it is generally though silently admitted that, while Charles Cotton came of a school of fishermen renowned for accomplishment even now, his master and friend was not in the modern or Cottonian sense a fisherman at all. There was in him, indeed, a vast deal of the philosopher and the observer of nature and still more, perhaps, of the artist in English; but there was also not a little of the cockney sportsman. He never rose above the low-lived worm and quill; his prey was commonly those fish that are the scorn of the true angler, for he knew naught of trout and grayling, yet was deeply interested in such base creatures (and such poor eating) as chub and roach and dace; and that part of his treatise which has still a certain authority—which may be said, indeed, to have placed the mystery of fly-fishing upon something of a scientific basis—was not his work but that of 'my most honoured friend, Charles Cotton, Esq.' Again, it is a characteristic of your true as opposed to your cockney sportsman that, unless constrained thereto by hunger, he does not eat what he has killed; and it is a characteristic of Walton—who in this particular at least may stand for the authentic type of the cockney sportsman as opposed to the true one—that he delighted not much less in dining or supping on his catch than he did in the act of making it: as witness some of the most charming parts in a book that from one end to the other is charm and little besides. Indeed the truth—(with reverence be it spoken)—appears to be that the *Compleat Angler* is an expression in the terms of art of the cit's enjoyment of the country.

Master Piscator.

What Walton saw in angling was not that delight in the consciousness of accomplishment and intelligence which sends the true fisherman to the river and keeps him there, rejoicing in his strength, whether he kill or go empty away. It was rather the pretext—with a worm and perhaps a good supper at one end and a contemplative man at the other—of a day in the fields: where the skylark soared, and the earth smelled sweet, and the water flashed and tinkled as it ran, while hard by some milk-maid, courteous yet innocent, sang as she plied her nimble fingers, and not very far away the casement of the inn-parlour gleamed comfortable promises of talk and food and rest. That was the Master Piscator who, being an excellent man of letters, went out to 'stretch his legs up Tottenham Hill' in search of fish, and came home with immortal copy; and that was the Izaak Walton who 'ventured to fill a part' of Cotton's 'margin' with remarks not upon his theory of how to angle for trout or grayling in a clear stream but 'by way of paraphrase for your reader's clearer understanding both of the situation of your fishing house, and the pleasantness of that you dwell in.' He had the purest and the most innocent of minds, he was the master of a style as bright, as sweet, as refreshing and delightful, as fine clean home-spun some time in lavender; he called himself an angler, and he believed in the description with a cordial simplicity whose appeal is more persuasive now than ever. But he was nothing if not the citizen afield—the cockney aweary of Bow Bells and rejoicing in 'the sights and sounds of the open landscape.' After all it is only your town-bred poet who knows anything of the country, or is moved to concern himself in anywise for the sensations and experiences it yields. Milton was born in Bread Street, and Herrick in Cheapside. Yet Milton gave us the *Allegro* and the *Penseroso* and the scenery in *Comus* and the epic; while as for Herrick—the *Night-Piece*, the lovely and immortal verses *To Meadows*, the fresh yet sumptuous and noble *To Corinna Going a-Maying*, these and a hundred more are there to answer for *him*. Here Walton is with Herrick and Milton and many 'dear sons of Memory' besides; and that is why he not only loved the country but was moved to make art of it as well.

HERRICK

His Muse.

In Herrick the air is fragrant with new-mown hay; there is a morning light upon all things; long shadows streak the grass, and on the eglantine swinging in the hedge the dew lies white and brilliant. Out of the happy distance comes a shrill and silvery sound of whetting scythes; and from the near brook-side rings the laughter of merry maids in circle to make cowslipballs and babble of their bachelors. As you walk you are conscious of 'the grace that morning meadows wear,' and mayhap you meet Amaryllis going home to the farm with an apronful of flowers. Rounded is she and buxom, cool-cheeked and vigorous and trim, smelling of rosemary and thyme, with an appetite for curds and cream and a tongue of 'cleanly wantonness.' For her singer has an eye in his head, and exquisite as are his fancies he dwells in no land of shadows. The more clearly he sees a thing the better he sings it; and provided that he do see it nothing is beneath the caress of his muse. The bays and rosemary that wreath the hall at Yule, the log itself, the Candlemas box, the hock-cart and the maypole, nay,

> 'See'st thou that cloud as silver clear,
> Plump, soft, and swelling everywhere?
> Tis Julia's bed!'—

And not only does he listen to the 'clecking' of his hen and know what it means: he knows too that the egg she has laid is long and white; so that ere he enclose it in his verse, you can see him take it in his hand, and look at it with a sort of boyish wonder and delight. This freshness of spirit, this charming and innocent curiosity, he carries into all he does. He can turn a sugared compliment with the best, but when Amaryllis passes him by he is yet so eager and unsophisticate that he can note that 'winning wave in the tempestuous petticoat' which has rippled to such good purpose through so many graceful speeches since. So that though Julia and Dianeme and Anthea have passed away, though Corinna herself is merely 'a fable, song, a fleeting shade,' he has saved enough of them from the ravin of Time for us to love and be grateful for eternally. Their gracious ghosts abide in a peculiar nook of the Elysium of Poesy. There 'in their habit as they lived' they dance in round, they fill their laps with flowers, they frolic and junket sweetly, they go for ever maying. Soft winds blow round them, and in their clear young voices they sing the verse of the rare artist who called them from the multitude and set them for ever where they are.

His Moral.

And Amaryllis herself will not, mayhap, be found so fair as those younglings of the year she bears with her in 'wicker ark' or 'lawny continent.' Herrick is pre-eminently the poet of flowers. He alone were capable of bringing back

> 'Le bouquet d'Ophélie
> De la rive inconnue où les flots l'ont laissé.

He knows and loves the dear blossoms all. He considers them with tender and shining eyes, he culls them his sweetest fancies and his fondest metaphors. Their idea is inseparable from that of his girls themselves, and it is by the means of the one set of mistresses that he is able so well to understand the other. The flowers are maids to him, and the maids are flowers. In an ecstasy of tender contemplation he turns from those to these, exampling Julia from the rose and pitying the hapless violets as though they were indeed not blooms insensitive but actually 'poor girls neglected.' His pages breathe their clean and innocent perfumes, and are beautiful with the chaste beauty of their colour, just as they carry with them something of the sweetness and simplicity of maidenhood itself. And from both he extracts the same pathetic little moral: both are lovely and both must die. And so, between his virgins that are for love indeed and those that sit silent and delicious in the 'flowery nunnery,' the old singer finds life so good a thing that he dreads to lose it, and not all his piety can remove the passionate regret with which he sees things hastening to their end.

His Piety.

That piety is equally removed from the erotic mysticism of Richard Crashaw and from the adoration, chastened and awful and pure, of Cowper. To find an analogue, you have to cross the borders of English into Spain. In his *Noble Numbers* Herrick shows himself to be a near kinsman of such men as Valdivielso, Ocaña, Lope de Ubeda; and there are versicles of his that in their homely mixture of the sacred and the profane, in their reverent familiarity with things divine, their pious and simple gallantry, may well be likened to the graceful and charming romances and villancicos of these strangers. Their spirit is less Protestant than Catholic, and is hardly English at all, so that it is scarce to be wondered at if they have remained unpopular. But their sincerity and earnestness are as far beyond doubt as their grace of line and inimitable daintiness of surface.

LOCKER

His Qualities.

Mr. Locker's verse has charmed so wisely and so long that it has travelled the full circle of compliment and exhausted one part of the lexicon of eulogy. As you turn his pages you feel as freshly as ever the sweet, old-world elegance, the courtly amiability, the mannerly restraint, the measured and accomplished ease. True, they are colourless, and in these days we are deboshed with colour; but then they are so luminously limpid and serene, they are so sprightly and graceful and gay! In the gallantry they affect there is a something at once exquisite and paternal. If they pun, 'tis with an air: even thus might Chesterfield have stooped to folly. And then, how clean the English, how light yet vigorous the touch, the manner how elegant and how staid! There is wit in them, and that so genial and unassuming that as like as not it gets leave to beam on unperceived. There is humour too, but humour so polite as to look half-unconscious, so dandified that it leaves you in doubt as to whether you should laugh or only smile. And withal there is a vein of well-bred wisdom never breathed but to the delight no less than to the profit of the student. And for those of them that are touched with passion, as in *The Unrealized Ideal* and that lovely odelet to Mabel's pearls, why, these are, I think, the best and the least approachable of all.

His Effect.

For as English as she is, indeed, his muse is not to be touched off save in French. To think of her is to reflect that she is *delicate, spirituelle, sémillante—une fine mouche, allez*! The *salon* has disappeared,—'Iran, indeed, is gone, and all his rose'; but she was born with the trick of it. You make your bow to her in her Sheraton chair, a buckle shoe engagingly discovered; and she rallies you with an incomparable ease, a delicate malice, in a dialect itself a distinction; and when she smiles it is behind or above a fan that points while it dissembles, that assists effect as delightfully as it veils intention. At times she is sensitive and tender, but her graver mood has no more of violence or mawkishness than has her gallant roguery (or enchanting archness) of viciousness or spite. Best of all, she is her poet's very own. You may woo her and pursue her as you will; but the end is invariable. 'I follow, follow still, but I shall never see her face.' Even as in her master's finest song.

BANVILLE

His Nature.

The Muse of M. de Banville was born not naked but in the most elaborate and sumptuous evening wear that ever muse put on. To him, indeed, there is no nature so natural as that depicted on the boards, no humanity half so human as the actor puts on with his paint. For him the flowers grow plucked and bound into nosegays; passion has no existence outside the Porte-Saint-Martin; the universe is a place of rhymes and rhythms, the human heart a supplement to the dictionary. He delights in babbling of green fields, and Homer, and Shakespeare, and the Eumenides, and the '*rire énorme*' of the *Frogs* and the *Lysistrata*. But it is suspected that he loves these things rather as words than as facts, and that in his heart of hearts he is better pleased with Cassandra and Columbine than with Rosalind and Othello, with the studio Hellas of Gautier than with the living Greece of Sophocles. Heroic objects are all very well in their way of course: they suggest superb effects in verse, they are of incomparable merit considered as colours and jewels for well-turned sentences in prose. But their function is purely verbal; they are the raw material of the outward form of poesy, and they come into being to glorify a climax, to adorn a refrain, to sparkle and sound in odelets and rondels and triolets, to twinkle and tinkle and chime all over the eight-and-twenty members of a fair ballade.

His Art.

It is natural enough that to a theory of art and life that can be thus whimsically described we should be indebted for some of the best writing of modern years. Our poet has very little sympathy with fact, whether heroic or the reverse, whether essential or accidental; but he is a rare artist in words and cadences. He writes of 'Pierrot, l'homme subtil,' and Columbine, and 'le beau Léandre,' and all the marionettes of that pleasant puppet-show which he mistakes for the world, with the rhetorical elegance and distinction, the verbal force and glow, the rhythmic beauty and propriety, of a rare poet; he models a group of flowers in wax as passionately and cunningly, and with as perfect an interest in the process and as lofty and august a faith in the result, as if he were carving the Venus of Milo, or scoring Beethoven's 'Fifth,' or producing *King Lear* or the *Ronde de Nuit*. He is profoundly artificial, but he is simple and even innocent in his artifice; so that he is often interesting and even affecting. He knows so well what should be done and so well how to do it that he not seldom succeeds in doing something that is actually and veritably art: something, that is, in which there is substance as well as form, in which the matter is equal with the manner, in which the imagination is human as well as æsthetic and the invention not merely verbal but emotional and romantic also. The dramatic and poetic value of such achievements in style as *Florise* and *Diane au Bois* is open to question; but there can be no doubt that *Gringoire* is a play. There is an abundance of 'epical ennui' in *le Sang de la Coupe* and *les Stalactites*; but the 'Nous n'irons plus au bois' and the charming epigram in which the poet paints a processional frieze of Hellenic virgins are high-water marks of verse. But, indeed, if Pierrot and Columbine were all the race, and the footlights might only change places with the sun, then were M. de Banville by way of being a Shakespeare.

DOBSON

Method and Effect.

 His style has distinction, elegance, urbanity, precision, an exquisite clarity. Of its kind it is as nearly as possible perfect. You think of Horace as you read; and you think of those among our own eighteenth century poets to whom Horace was an inspiration and an example. The epithet is usually so just that it seems to have come into being with the noun it qualifies; the metaphor is mostly so appropriate that it leaves you in doubt as to whether it suggested the poem or the poem suggested it; the verb is never in excess of the idea it would convey; the effect of it all is that 'something has here got itself uttered,' and for good. Could anything, for instance, be better, or less laboriously said, than this poet's remonstrance *To an Intrusive Butterfly*? The thing is instinct with delicate observation, so aptly and closely expressed as to seem natural and living as the facts observed:

> 'I watch you through the garden walks,
> I watch you *float* between
> The *avenues* of dahlia stalks,
> And *flicker* on the green;

You *hover* round the garden seat,
  You *mount*, you *waver*. . .

* * * * *

Across the room *in loops of flight*
  I watch you wayward go;
* * * * *
Before the bust you flaunt and flit—
* * * * *
You *pause*, you *poise*, you *circle up*
  Among my old Japan.'

And all the rest of it. The theme is but the vagaries of a wandering insect; but how just and true is the literary instinct, how perfect the literary *savoir-faire*! The words I have italicised are the only words (it seems) in the language that are proper to the occasion; and yet how quietly they are produced, with what apparent unconsciousness they are set to do their work, how just and how sufficient is their effect! In writing of this sort there is a certain artistic good-breeding whose like is not common in these days. We have lost the secret of it: we are too eager to make the most of our little souls in art and too ignorant to do the best by them; too egoistic and 'individual,' too clever and skilful and well informed, to be content with the completeness of simplicity. Even the Laureate was once addicted to glitter for glitter's sake; and with him to keep them in countenance there is a thousand minor poets whose 'little life' is merely a giving way to the necessities of what is after all a condition of intellectual impotence but poorly redeemed by a habit of artistic swagger. The singer of Dorothy and Beau Brocade is of another race. He is 'the co-mate and brother in exile' of Matthew Arnold and the poet of *The Unknown Eros*. Alone among modern English bards they stand upon that ancient way which is the best: attentive to the pleadings of the Classic Muse, heedful always to give such thoughts as they may breed no more than their due expression.

BERLIOZ

The Critic.

One of the very few great musicians who have been able to write their own language with vigour and perspicuity, Berlioz was for many years among the kings of the feuilleton, among the most accomplished journalists of the best epoch of the Parisian press. He had an abundance of wit and humour; his energy and spirit were inexhaustible; within certain limits he was a master of expression and style; in criticism as in music he was an artist to his finger-ends; and if he found writing hard work what he wrote is still uncommonly easy reading. He is one of the few—the very few—journalists the worth of whose achievement has been justified by collection and republication. Louis Veuillot has been weighed in this balance, and found wanting; and so has Janin prince of critics. With Berlioz it is otherwise. If you are no musician he appeals to you as a student of life; if you are interested in life and music both he is irresistible. The *Mémoires* is one of the two or three essays in artistic biography which may claim equal honours with Benvenuto's story of himself and his own doings; the two volumes of correspondence rank with the most interesting epistolary matter of these times; in the *Grotesques*, the *A Travers Chants*, the *Soirées de l'Orchestre* there is enough of fun and earnest, of fine criticism and diabolical humour, of wit and fancy and invention, to furnish forth a dozen ordinary critics, and leave a rich remainder when all's done. These books have been popular for years; they are popular still; and the reason is not far to seek. Berlioz was not only a great musician and a brilliant writer; he was also a very interesting and original human being. His writings are one expression of an abnormal yet very natural individuality; and when he speaks you are sure of something worth hearing and remembering.

A Prototype.

Apart from Cellini's ruffianism there are several points of contact between the two men. Berlioz made the roaring goldsmith the hero of an opera, and it is not doubtful that he was in complete sympathy with his subject. In the Frenchman there is a full measure of the waywardness of temper, the impatience of authority, the resolute and daring humour, the passion of worship for what is great in art and of contempt for what is little and bad, which entered so largely into the composition of the Florentine. There is not much to choose between the Berlioz of the *Débats*, the author of the *Grotesques de la Musique* and the *A Travers Chants*, and the Benvenuto who, as Il Lasca writes of him,

Views and Reviews

'Senza alcun ritegno o barbazzale
Delle cose malfatte dicea male.'

Benvenuto enlarges upon the joys of drawing from the life and expatiates upon the greatness of Michelangelo in much the same spirit and with much the same fury of admiration with which Berlioz descants upon the rapture of conducting an orchestra and dilates upon the beauty of *Divinités du Styx* or the adagio of the so-called *Moonlight Sonata*. It is written of Benvenuto, in connection with Vasari's attack upon that cupola of Santa Maria del Fiore which himself was wont to call 'the marvel of beautiful things,' that if he had lived to see the result,

'Certo non capirebbe nelle pelle;
E saltando, e correndo, e fulminando,
S' andrebbe querelando,
E per tutto gridando ad alta voce
Giorgin d'Arezzo meterebbe in croce,
Oggi universalmente
Odiato della gente
Quasi publico ladro e assassino';

and you are reminded irresistibly of Berlioz betrampling Lachnith and the ingenious Castil-Blaze and defending Beethoven against the destructive pedantry of Fétis. And, just as the *Vita* is invaluable as a personal record of artist-life in the Italy of the Renaissance, so are the *Mémoires* invaluable as a personal record of the works and ways of musicians in the Paris of the Romantic revival. Berlioz is revealed in them for one of the race of the giants. He is the musician of 1830, as Delacroix is the painter; and his work is as typical and as significant as the *Sardanapale* and the *Faust* lithographs.

His Theory of Autobiography.

To read the *Mémoires* is to feel that in writing them the great musician deliberately set himself to win the heart of posterity. He believed in himself, and he believed in his music: he divined that one day or another he would be legendary as well as immortal; and he took an infinite deal of pains to make certain that the ideal which was presently to represent him in men's minds should be an ideal of which he could thoroughly approve. It is fair to note that in this care for the good will and the good word of the future he was not by any means alone. The *romantiques*, indeed, were keen—from Napoleon downwards—to make the very best of themselves. The poet of the *Légende des Siècles*, for example, went early to work to arrange the story of his life and character at least as carefully as he composed the audiences of his *premières*; and he did it with so light a hand, and with such a sense of the importance of secrecy, that it is even now by no means so well and widely known as it should be that *Victor Hugo raconté par un Témoin de sa Vie* is the work of the hero's wife, and was not only inspired but may also have been revised and prepared for publication by the hero himself. Again, the dramatist of *Antony* and the novelist of *Bragelonne* was never so happy as when he was engaged upon the creation of what he hoped would be the historical Dumas; he made volume after volume of delightful reading out of his own impressions and adventures; he turned himself into copy with a frankness, a grace, a gusto, a persistency of egoism, which are merely enchanting. Berlioz, therefore, had good warrant for his work. It is more to the point, perhaps, that he would have taken it if he had not had it. And I hold that he would have done well; for (in any case) a great man's notion of himself is, *ipso facto*, better and more agreeable and convincing, especially as he presents it, than the idea of his inferiors and admirers, especially as presented by them. Berlioz, it is true, was prodigal in these *Mémoires* of his of wit and fun and devilry, of fine humanity and noble art, of good things said and great things dreamed and done and suffered; but he was prodigal of invention and suppression as well, and the result, while considerably less veracious, is all the more fascinating, therefor. One feels that for one thing he was too complete an artist to be merely literal and exact; that for another he saw and felt things for himself, as Milton did before him—Milton in the mind's eye of Milton the noblest of created things and to Mr. Saintsbury almost as unpleasing a spectacle as the gifted but abject Racine; and for a third that from his own point of view he was right, and there is an end of it.

GEORGE ELIOT

The Ideal.

It was thought that with George Eliot the Novel-with-a-Purpose had really come to be an adequate instrument for the regeneration of humanity. It was understood that Passion only survived to point a moral or provide the materials of an awful tale, while Duty, Kinship, Faith, were so far paramount as to govern Destiny and mould the world. A vague, decided flavour of Liberty, Equality, and Fraternity was felt to pervade the moral universe, a chill but seemly halo of Golden Age was seen to play soberly about things in general. And it was with confidence anticipated that those perfect days were on the march when men and women would propose—(from the austerest motives)—by the aid of scientific terminology.

The Real.

To the Sceptic—(an apostate, and an undoubted male)—another view was preferable. He held that George Eliot had carried what he called the 'Death's-Head Style' of art a trifle too far. He read her books in much the same spirit and to much the same purpose that he went to the gymnasium and diverted himself with parallel bars. He detested her technology; her sententiousness revolted while it amused him; and when she put away her puppets and talked of them learnedly and with understanding—instead of letting them explain themselves, as several great novelists have been content to do—he recalled how Wisdom crieth out in the street and no man regardeth her, and perceived that in this case the fault was Wisdom's own. He accepted with the humility of ignorance, and something of the learner's gratitude, her woman generally, from Romola down to Mrs. Pullet. But his sense of sex was strong enough to make him deny the possibility in any stage of being of nearly all the governesses in revolt it pleased her to put forward as men; for with very few exceptions he knew they were heroes of the divided skirt. To him Deronda was an incarnation of woman's rights; Tito an 'improper female in breeches'; Silas Marner a good, perplexed old maid, of the kind of whom it is said that they have 'had a disappointment.' And Lydgate alone had aught of the true male principle about him.

Appreciations.

Epigrams are at best half-truths that look like whole ones. Here is a handful about George Eliot. It has been said of her books—('on several occasions')—that 'it is doubtful whether they are novels disguised as treatises, or treatises disguised as novels'; that, 'while less romantic than Euclid's

Elements, they are on the whole a great deal less improving reading'; and that 'they seem to have been dictated to a plain woman of genius by the ghost of David Hume.' Herself, too, has been variously described: as 'An Apotheosis of Pupil-Teachery'; as 'George Sand *plus* Science and *minus* Sex'; as 'Pallas with prejudices and a corset'; as 'the fruit of a caprice of Apollo for the Differential Calculus.' The comparison of her admirable talent to 'not the imperial violin but the grand ducal violoncello' seems suggestive and is not unkind.

BORROW

His Vocation.

Three hundred years since Borrow would have been a gentleman adventurer: he would have dropped quietly down the river, and steered for the Spanish Main, bent upon making carbonadoes of your Don. But he came too late for that, and falling upon no sword and buckler age but one that was interested in Randal and Spring, he accepted that he found, and did his best to turn its conditions, into literature. As he had that admirable instinct of making the best of things which marks the true adventurer, he was on the whole exceeding happy. There was no more use in sailing for Javan and Gadire; but at home there were highways in abundance, and what is your genuine tramp but a dry-land sailor? The Red Man is exhausted of everything but sordidness; but under that round-shouldered little tent at the bend of the road, beside that fire artistically built beneath that kettle of the comfortable odours, among those horses and colts at graze hard by, are men and women more mysterious and more alluring to the romantic mind than any Mingo or Comanch that ever traded a scalp. While as for your tricks of fence—your immortal *passado*, your *punto reverso*—if that be no longer the right use for a gentleman, have not

Views and Reviews

Spring and Langan fought their great battle on Worcester racecourse? and has not Cribb of Gloucestershire—that renowned, heroic, irresistible Thomas—beaten Molyneux the negro artist in the presence of twenty thousand roaring Britons? and shall the practice of an art which has rejoiced in such a master as the illustrious Game Chicken, Hannibal of the Ring, be held degrading by an Englishman of sufficient inches who, albeit a Tory and a High Churchman, is at bottom as thoroughgoing a Republican as ever took the word of command from Colonel Cromwell? And if all this fail, if he get nobody to put on the gloves with him, if the tents of the Romany prove barren of interest, if the king's highway be vacant of adventure as Mayfair, he has still philology to fall back upon, he can still console himself with the study of strange tongues, he can still exult in a peculiar superiority by quoting the great Ab Gwylim where the baser sort of persons is content with Shakespeare. So that what with these and some kindred diversions—a little horse-whispering and ale-drinking, the damnation of Popery, the study of the Bible—he can manage not merely to live but to live so fully and richly as to be the envy of some and the amazement of all. That, as life goes and as the world wags, is given to few. Add to it the credit of having written as good a book about Spain as ever was written in any language, the happiness of having dreamed and partly lived that book ere it was written, the perfect joy of being roundly abused by everybody, and the consciousness of being different from everybody and of giving at least as good as ever you got at several things the world is silly enough to hold in worship—as the Toryism of Sir Walter, or the niceness of Popery, or the pleasures of Society: and is it not plain that Borrow was a man uncommon fortunate, and that he enjoyed life as greatly as most men not savages who have possessed the fruition of this terrestrial sphere?

Ideals and Achievements.

He prepared his effects as studiously and almost as dexterously as Dumas himself. His instinct of the picturesque was rarely indeed at fault; he marshalled his personages and arranged his scene with something of that passion for effect which entered so largely into the theory of M. le Comte de Monte-Cristo. However closely disguised, himself is always the heroic figure, and he is ever busy in arranging discovery and triumph. To his chance-mates he is but an eccentric person, an amateur tinker, a slack-baked gipsy, an unlettered hack; to his audience he is his own, strong, indifferent self: presently the rest will recognise him and he will be disdainfully content. And recognise him they do. He throws off his disguise; there is a gape, a stare, a general conviction that Lavengro is the greatest man in the world; and then—as the manner of Lesage commands—the adventure ends, the stars resume their wonted courses, and the self-conscious Tinker-Quixote takes the road once more and passes on to other achievements: a mad preacher to succour, a priest to baffle, some tramp to pound into a jelly of humility, an applewoman to mystify, a horse-chaunter to swindle, a pugilist to study and help and portray. But whatever it be, Lavengro emerges from the ordeal modestly, unobtrusively, quietly, most consciously magnificent. Circumstantial as Defoe, rich in combinations as Lesage, and with such an instinct of the picturesque, both personal and local, as none of these possessed, this strange wild man holds on his strange wild way, and leads you captive to the end. His dialogue is copious and appropriate: you feel that like Ben Jonson he is dictating rather than reporting, that he is less faithful and exact than imaginative and determined; but you are none the less pleased with it, and suspicious though you be that the voice is Lavengro's and the hands are the hands of some one else, you are glad to surrender to the illusion, and you regret when it is dispelled. Moreover, that all of it should be set down in racy, nervous, idiomatic English, with a kind of eloquence at once primitive and scholarly, precious but homely—the speech of an artist in sods and turfs—if at first it surprise and charm yet ends by seeming so natural and just that you go on to forget all about it and accept the whole thing as the genuine outcome of a man's experience which it purports to be. Add that it is all entirely unsexual; that there is none with so poor an intelligence of the heart as woman moves it; that the book does not exist in which the relations between boy and girl are more miserably misrepresented than in *Lavengro* and *The Romany Rye*; that that picaresque ideal of romance which, finding utterance in Hurtado de Mendoza, was presently to appeal to such artists as Cervantes, Quevedo, Lesage, Smollett, the Dickens of *Pickwick*, finds such expression in *Lavengro* and *The Romany Rye* as nowhere else; and the tale of Borrow is complete enough.

Himself.

Despite or because of a habit of mystification which obliged him to jumble together the homely Real and a not less homely Ideal, Lavengro will always, I think, be found worthy of companionship, if only as the one exemplary artist-tramp the race has yet achieved. The artist-tramp, the tinker who can write, the horse-coper with a twang of Hamlet and a habit of Monte-Cristo—that is George Borrow. For them that love these differences there is none in whom they are so cunningly and quaintly blended as George Borrow; and they that love them not may keep the other side of the road and fare in peace elsewhither.

BALZAC

Under which King?

To Goethe it seemed that every one of Balzac's novels had been dug out of a suffering woman's heart: but Goethe spoke not always wisely, and in this exacting world there be some that not only have found fault with Balzac's method and results but have dared to declare his theory of society the dream of a mind diseased. To these critics Balzac was less observer than creator: his views were false, his vision was distorted, and though he had 'incomparable power' he had not power enough to make them accept his work. This theory is English, and in France they find Balzac possible enough. There is something of him in Pierre Dupont; he made room for the work of Flaubert, Feydeau, the younger Dumas, Augier and Zola and the brothers Goncourt; and to him Charles Baudelaire is as some fat strange fungus to the wine-cask in whose leakings it springs. Sainte-Beuve refused to accept him, but his 'Pigault-Lebrun des duchesses' is only malicious: he resented the man's exuberant and inordinate personality, and made haste to apply to it some drops of that sugared vitriol of which he had the secret. Taine is a fitter critic of the *Comédie humaine* than Sainte-Beuve; and Taine has come to other conclusions. Acute, coarse, methodical, exhaustive, he has recognised the greatness of one still more exhaustive, methodical, coarse, and acute than himself. English critics fall foul of Balzac's women; but Taine falls foul of English critics, and with the authority of a Parisian by profession declares that the *Parisiennes* of the *Comédie* are everything they ought to be—the true daughters of their 'bon gros libertin de père.' And while Taine, exulting in his Marneffe and his Coralie, does solemnly and brilliantly show that he is right and everybody else is wrong, a later writer—English of course—can find no better parallel of Balzac than Browning, and knows nothing in art so like the Pauline of *la Peau de Chagrin* as the Sistine Madonna. It is curious, this clash of opinions; and it is plain that one or other party must be wrong. Which is it? 'Qui trompe-t-on ici?' Is Taine a better judge than Mr. Leslie Stephen or Mr. Henry James? Or are Messrs. James and Stephen better qualified to speak with authority than Taine? It may be that none but a Frenchman can thoroughly and intimately apprehend in its inmost a thing so essentially French as the *Comédie*; it is a fact that Frenchmen of all sorts and sizes have accepted the *Comédie* in its totality; and that is reason good enough for any commonplace Englishman who is lacking in the vanity of originality to accept it also.

The Fact.

Balzac's ambition was to be omnipotent. He would be Michelangelesque, and that by sheer force of minuteness. He exaggerated scientifically, and made things gigantic by a microscopic fulness of detail. His Hulot was to remain the Antony of modern romance, losing the world for the love of woman, and content to lose it; his Marneffe, in whom is incarnated the instinct and the science of sexual corruption, is Hulot's Cleopatra, and only dies because 'elle va faire le bon Dieu'—as who should say 'to mash the Old Man'; Frenhœffer, Philippe Bridau, Vautrin, Marsay, Rastignac, Grandet, Balthazar Claës, Béatrix, Sarrazine, Lousteau, Esther, Lucien Chardon—the list is, I believe, some thousands strong! Also the argument is proved in advance: there is the *Comédie* itself—'the new edition fifty volumes long.' Bad or good, foul or fair, impossible or actual, a monstrous debauch of mind or a triumph of realisation, there is the *Comédie*. It is forty years since Balzac squared and laid the last stones of it; and it exists—if a little the worse for wear: the bulk is enormous—if the materials be in some sort worm-eaten and crumbling. Truly, he had 'incomparable power.' He was the least capable and the most self-conscious of artists; his observation was that of an inspired and very careful auctioneer; he was a visionary and a fanatic; he was gross, ignorant, morbid of mind, cruel in heart, vexed with a strain of Sadism that makes him on the whole corrupting and ignoble in effect. But he divined and invented prodigiously if he observed and recorded tediously, and his achievement remains a phantasmagoria of desperate suggestions and strange, affecting situations and potent and inordinate effects. He may be impossible; but there is French literature and French society to show that he passed that way, and had 'incomparable power.' The phrase is Mr. Henry James's, and it is hard to talk of Balzac and refrain from it.

LABICHE

Teniers or Daumier?

To the maker of Poirier and Fabrice, of Séraphine and Giboyer, of Olympe and the Marquis d'Auberive, there were analogies between the genius of Labiche and the genius of Teniers. 'C'est au premier abord,' says he, 'le même aspect de caricature; c'est, en y regardant de plus près, la même finesse de tons, la même justesse d'expression, la même vivacité de mouvement.' For myself, I like to think of Labiche as in some sort akin to Honoré Daumier. Earnestness and accomplishment apart, he has much in common with that king of caricaturists. The lusty frankness, the jovial ingenuity, the keen sense of the ridiculous, the insatiable instinct of observation, of the draughtsman are a great part of the equipment of the playwright. Augier notes that truth is everywhere in Labiche's work, and Augier is right. He is before everything a dramatist: an artist, that is, whose function is to tell a story in action and by the mouths of its personages; and whimsical and absurd as he loves to be, he is never either the one or the other at the expense of nature. He is often careless and futile: he will squander—(as in *Vingt-neuf Degrés à l'Ombre* and *l'Avare en Gants Jaunes*)—an idea that rightly belongs to the domain of pure comedy on the presentation of a most uproarious farce. But he is never any falser to his vocation than this. Now and then, as in *Moi* and *le Voyage de M. Perrichon*, he is an excellent comic poet, dealing with comedy seriously as comedy should be dealt with, and incarnating a vice or an affectation in a certain character with impeccable justness and assurance. Now and then, as in *les Petits Oiseaux* and *les Vivacités du Capitaine Tic*, he is content to tell a charming story as pleasantly as possible. Sometimes, as in *Célimare le Bien-Aimé* (held by M. Sarcey to be the high-water mark of the modern *vaudeville*), *le Plus Heureux des Trois*, and *le Prix Martin*, he fights again from a humouristic point of view that triangular duel between the wife, the husband, and the lover which fills so large a place in the literature of France; and then he shows the reverse of the medal of adultery—with the husband at his ease, the seducer haunted by the ghosts of old sins, the erring wife the slave of her unsuspecting lord. Or again, he takes to turning the world upside down, and—as in the *Cagnotte*, the *Chapeau de Paille*, and the *Trente Millions*—to producing a scheme of morals and society that seems to have been dictated from an Olympus demoralised by champagne and lobster. But at his wildest he never forgets that men and women are themselves. His dialogue is always right and appropriate, however extravagant it be. His vivid and varied knowledge of life and character supplies him with touches enough of nature and truth to make the fortune of a dozen ordinary dramatists; and withal you feel as you read that he is writing, as Augier says of him, to amuse himself merely, and that he could an if he would be solemn and didactic with all the impressiveness that a perfect acquaintance with men and things and an admirable dramatic aptitude can bestow. The fact that he is always in a good temper has done him some wrong in that it has led him to be to all appearances amusing only, where he might well have posed as a severe and serious artist. But he is none the less true for having elected to be funny, and there is certainly more genuine human nature and human feeling in such drolleries as the *Chapeau de Paille* and *le Plus Heureux des Trois* than in all the serious dramas of Ponsard (say) and Hugo put together.

Labiche.

Perhaps the most characteristic and individual part of his work is that in which he has given his invention full swing, and allowed his humour to play its maddest pranks at will. *Moi* is an admirable comedy, and De la Porcheraie is almost hideously egoistic; the *Voyage de M. Perrichon* is delightful reading, and Perrichon is as pompous an ass as I know; but the *Chapeau de Paille*, the *Cagnotte*, the *Trente Millions*, the *Sensitive*, the *Deux Merles Blancs*, the *Doit-On le Dire*, and their compeers—with them it is other-guess work altogether. In these whimsical phantasmagorias men and women move and speak as at the bidding of destinies drunk with laughing-gas. Time and chance have gone demented, fate has turned comic poet, society has become its own parody, everybody is the irrepressible caricature of himself. You are in a topsy-turvy world, enveloped in an atmosphere instinct with gaiety and folly, where burlesque is natural and only the extravagant is normal; where your Chimæra has grown frolic, your Nightmare is first Cousin to the Cheshire Cat, and your Sphinxes are all upon the spree; and where you have as little concern for what is real as you have in that hemisphere of the great globe of Molière—that has Scapin and Sganarelle for its breed-bates, and Pourceaugnac for its butt, and Pancrace and Marphurius for its scientific men, and Lélie and Agnès for its incarnations of love and beauty. That the creator of such a world as this should have aspired to the Academy's spare arm-chair—that one above all others but just vacated by the respectable M. de Sacy—was a fact that roused the *Revue des Deux Mondes* even to satire. But if the arm-chair brought honour with it, then no man better deserved the privilege than Eugène Labiche, for he had amused and kept awake the public for nearly forty years—for almost as long, that is, as the *Revue* had been sending it to sleep. There are times and seasons when a good laugh makes more for edification than whole folios of good counsel. 'I regarded him not,' quoth Sir John of one that would have moved him to sapience, 'and yet he talked wisely.' Now Sir

Views and Reviews

John, whatever his opinion of the *Revue*, would never have said all that—the second part of it he might—of anything signed 'Eugène Labiche,' nor—so I love to believe—would his august creator either. For is not his work so full of quick, fiery, and delectable shapes as to be perpetual sherris? And when time and season fit, what more can the heart of man desire?

CHAMPFLEURY

The Man.

Champfleury—novelist, dramatist, archæologist, humourist, and literary historian—belonged to a later generation than that of Petrus Borel and Philothée O'Neddy; but he could remember the production of *les Burgraves*, and was able of his own personal knowledge to laugh at the melancholy speech of poor Célestin Nanteuil—the famous 'Il n'y a plus de jeunesse' of a man grown old and incredulous and apathetic before his time: the lament over a yesterday already a hundred years behind. He had lived in the Latin quarter; he had dined with Flicoteaux, and listened to the orchestras of Habeneck and Musard; he had heard the chimes at midnight with Baudelaire and Murger, hissed the tragedies of Ponsard, applauded Deburau and Rouvière, and seen the rise and fall of Courbet and Dupont. If he was not of the giants he was of their immediate successors, and he had seen them actually at work. He had hacked for Balzac, and read romantic prose at Victor Hugo's; he had lived so near the red waistcoat of Théophile Gautier as to dare to go up and down in Paris (under the inspiration of the artist of *la Femme qui taille la Soupe*) in 'un habit en bouracan vert avec col à la Marat, un gilet de couleur bachique, et une culotte en drap d'un jaune assez malséant,' together with 'une triomphante cravate de soie jaune'—a vice of Baudelaire's inventing—and 'un feutre ras dans le goût de la coiffure de Camille Desmoulins.' And having seen for himself, he could judge for himself as well. From first to last he showed himself to be out of sympathy with the ambitions and effects of romanticism. He was born a humourist and an observer, and he became a 'realist' as soon as he began to write.

The Writer.

His work is an antipodes not only of *Hernani* and *Notre-Dame* but of *Sarrazine* and *la Cousine Bette* and *Béatrix* as well. For the commonplace types and incidents, the everyday passions and fortunes, of the *Aventures de Mariette* and the *Mascarade de la Vie Parisienne* represent a reaction not alone against the sublimities and the extravagance of Hugo but against the heroic aggrandisement of things trivial of Balzac as well. True, they deal with kindred subjects, and they purport to be a record of life as it is and not of life as it ought to be. But the pupil's point of view is poles apart from the master's; his intention, his ambition, his inspiration, belong to another order of ideas. He contents himself with observing and noting and reflecting; with making prose prosaic and adding sobriety and plainness to a plain and sober story; with being merely curious and intelligent; with using experience not as an intoxicant but as a staple of diet; with considering fact not as the raw material of inspiration but as inspiration itself. Between an artist of this sort—pedestrian, good-tempered, touched with malice, a little cynical—and the noble desperadoes of 1830 there could be little sympathy; and there seems no reason why the one should be the others' historian, and none why, if their historian he should be, his history should be other than partial and narrow—than at best an achievement in special pleading. But Champfleury's was a personality apart. His master quality was curiosity; he was interested in everything, and he was above all things interested in men and women; he had a liberal mind and no prejudices; he had the scientific spirit and the scientific intelligence, if he sometimes spoke with the voice of the humourist and in the terms of the artist in words; and his studies in romanticism are far better literature than his experiments in fiction.

LONGFELLOW

Sea Poets.

The ocean as confidant, a Laertes that can neither avoid his Hamlets nor bid them hold their peace, is a modern invention. Byron and Shelley discovered it; Heine took it into his confidence, and told it the story of his loves; Wordsworth made it a moral influence; Browning loved it in his way, but his way was not often the poet's; to Matthew Arnold it was the voice of destiny, and its message was a message of despair; Hugo conferred with it as with an humble friend, and uttered such lofty things over it as are rarely heard upon the lips of man. And so with living lyrists each after his kind. Lord Tennyson listens and looks until it strikes him out an undying note of passion, or yearning, or regret—

'Sunset and evening star,
And one clear call for me';

Mr. Swinburne maddens with the wind and the sounds and the scents of it, until there passes into his verse a something of its vastness and its vehemency, the rapture of its inspiration, the palpitating, many-twinkling miracle of its light; Mr. William Morris has been taken with the manner of its melancholy; while to Whitman it has been 'the great Camerado' indeed, for it gave him that song of the brown bird bereft of his mate in whose absence the half of him had not been told to us.

Longfellow.

But to Longfellow alone was it given to see that stately galley which Count Arnaldos saw; his only to hear the steersman singing that wild and wondrous song which none that hears it can resist, and none that has heard it may forget. Then did he learn the old monster's secret—the word of his charm, the core of his mystery, the human note in his music, the quality of his influence upon the heart and the mind of man; and then did he win himself a place apart among sea poets. With the most of them it is a case of *Ego et rex meus*: It is I and the sea, and my egoism is as valiant and as vocal as the other's. But Longfellow is the spokesman of a confraternity; what thrills him to utterance is the spirit of that strange and beautiful freemasonry established as long ago as when the first sailor steered the first keel out into the unknown, irresistible water-world, and so established the foundations of the eternal brotherhood of man with ocean. To him the sea is a place of mariners and ships. In his verse the rigging creaks, the white sail fills and crackles, there are blown smells of pine and hemp and tar; you catch the home wind on your cheeks; and old shipmen, their eyeballs white in their bronzed faces, with silver rings and gaudy handkerchiefs, come in and tell you moving stories of the immemorial, incommunicable deep. He abides in a port; he goes down to the docks, and loiters among the galiots and brigantines, he hears the melancholy song of the chanty-men; he sees the chips flying under the shipwright's adze; he smells the pitch that smokes and bubbles in the caldron. And straightway he falls to singing his variations on the ballad of Count Arnaldos; and the world listens, for its heart beats in his song.

TENNYSON

St. Agnes' Eve.

In Keats's *St. Agnes' Eve* nothing is white but the heroine. It is winter, and 'bitter chill'; the hare 'limps trembling through the frozen grass; the owl is a-cold for all his feathers; the beadsman's fingers are numb, his breath is frosted; and at an instant of special and peculiar romance

> 'The frost-wind blows
> Like Love's alarum, pattering the sharp sleet
> Against the window-panes.'

But there is no snow. The picture is pure colour: it blushes with blood of queens and kings; it glows with 'splendid dyes,' like the 'tiger-moth's deep-damasked wings'—with 'rose bloom,' and warm gules,' and 'soft amethyst'; it is loud with music and luxurious with 'spiced dainties,' with lucent syrops tinct with cinnamon,' with 'manna and dates,' the fruitage of Fez and 'cedared Lebanon' and 'silken Samarcand.' Now, the Laureate's *St. Agnes' Eve* is an ecstasy of colourless perfection. The snows sparkle on the convent roof; the 'first snowdrop' vies with St. Agnes' virgin bosom;

the moon shines an 'argent round' in the 'frosty skies'; and in a transport of purity the lady prays:

> 'Break up thy heavens, O Lord! and far,
>   Through all the starlight keen,
>   Draw me thy bride, a glittering star,
>   In raiment white and clean.'

It is all coldly, miraculously stainless: as somebody has said, 'la vraie *Symphonie en Blanc Majeur.*'

Indian Summer.

And at four-score the poet of *St. Agnes' Eve* is still our greatest since the Wordsworth of certain sonnets and the two immortal odes: is still the one Englishman of whom it can be stated and believed that Elisha is not less than Elijah. His verse is far less smooth and less lustrous than in the well-filed times of *In Memoriam* and the Arthurian idylls. But it is also far more plangent and affecting; it shows a larger and more liberal mastery of form and therewith a finer, stronger, saner sentiment of material; in its display of breadth and freedom in union with particularity, of suggestiveness with precision, of swiftness of handling with completeness of effect, it reminds you of the later magic of Rembrandt and the looser and richer, the less artful-seeming but more ample and sumptuous, of the styles of Shakespeare. And the matter is worthy of the manner. Everywhere are greatness and a high imagination moving at ease in the gold armour of an heroic style. There are passages in *Demeter and Persephone* that will vie with the best in *Lucretius*; *Miriam* is worth a wilderness of *Aylmer's Fields*; *Owd Roä* is one of the best of the studies in dialect; in *Happy* there are stanzas that recall the passion of *Rizpah*; nothing in modern English so thrills and vibrates with the prophetic inspiration, the fury of the seer, as *Vastness*; the verses *To Mary Boyle*—(in the same stanza as Musset's *le Mie Prigioni*)—are marked by such a natural grace of form and such a winning 'affectionateness,' to coin a word, of intention and accomplishment as Lord Tennyson has never surpassed nor very often equalled. In *Vastness* the insight into essentials, the command of primordial matter, the capacity of vital suggestion, are gloriously in evidence from the first line to the last. Here is no touch of ingenuity, no trace of 'originality,' no single sign of cleverness; the rhymes are merely inevitable—there is no visible transformation of metaphor in deference to their suggestions; nothing is antic, peculiar, superfluous; but here in epic unity and completeness, here is a sublimation of experience expressed by means of a sublimation of style. It is unique in English, and for all that one can see it is like to remain unique this good while yet. The impression you take is one of singular loftiness of purpose and a rare nobility of mind. Looking upon life and time and the spirit of man from the heights of his eighty years, it has been given to the Master Poet to behold much that is hid to them in the plain or on the slopes beneath him, and beholding it to frame and utter a message so lofty in style and in significance so potent that it sounds as of this world indeed but from the confines of experience, the farthest kingdoms of mortality.

His Mastership.

It is to note, too, that the Laureate of to-day deals with language in a way that to the Tennyson of the beginning was—unhappily—impossible. In those early years he neither would nor could have been responsible for the magnificent and convincing rhythms of *Vastness*, the austere yet passionate shapeliness of *Happy*, the effects of vigour and variety realised in *Parnassus*. For in those early years he was rather Benvenuto than Michelangelo, he was more of a jeweller than a sculptor, the phrase was too much to him, the inspiration of the incorrect too little. All that is changed, and for the best. Most interesting is it to the artist to remark how impatient—(as the Milton of the *Agonistes* was)—of rhyme and how confident in rhythm is the whilome poet of *Oriana* and *The Lotus-Eaters* and *The Vision of Sin*; and how this impatience and this confidence are revealed not merely in a piece of mysticism naked yet unashamed as *The*

Gleam—(whose movement with its constancy in double endings and avoidance of triplets is perhaps a little tame)—but also in what should have been a popular piece: the ode, to wit, *On the Jubilee of Queen Victoria*. In eld, indeed, the craftsman inclines to play with his material: he is conscious of mastery; he is in the full enjoyment of his own; he indulges in experiments which to him are as a crown of glory and to them that come after him—to the noodles that would walk in his ways without first preparing themselves by prayer and study and a life of abnegation—are only the devil in disguise. The Rembrandt of *The Syndics*, the Shakespeare of *The Tempest* and *Lear*—what are these but pits for the feet of the Young Ass? and what else will be the Tennyson of *Vastness* and *The Gleam*? 'Lord,' quoth Dickens years ago in respect of the *Idylls* or of *Maud*, 'what a pleasure it is to come across a man that can *write*!' He also was an artist in words; and what he said then he would say now with greater emphasis and more assurance. From the first Lord Tennyson has been an exemplar; and now in these new utterances, his supremacy is completely revealed. There is no fear now that 'All will grow the flower, For all have got the seed'; for then it was a mannerism that people took and imitated, and now—! Now it is art; it is the greater Shakespeare, the consummate Rembrandt, the unique Velasquez; and they may rise to it that can.

GORDON HAKE

Aim and Equipment.

Dr. Hake is one of the most earnest and original of poets. He has taken nothing from his contemporaries, but has imagined a message for himself, and has chosen to deliver it in terms that are wholly his own. For him the accidents and trivialities of individualism, the transitory and changing facts that make up the external aspect of an age or a character, can hardly be said to exist. He only concerns himself with absolutes—the eternal elements of human life and the immutable tides of human destiny. It is of these that the stuff of his message is compacted; it is from these that its essence is distilled. His talk is not of Arthur and Guinevere, nor Chastelard and Atalanta, nor Paracelsus and Luria and Abt Vogler; of 'the drawing-room and the deanery' he has nothing to say; nothing of the tendencies of Strauss and Renan, nothing of the New Renaissance, nothing of Botticelli, nor the ballet, nor the text of Shakespeare, nor the joys of the book-hunter, nor the quaintness of Queen Anne, nor the morals of Helen of Troy. To these he prefers the mystery of death, the significance of life, the quality of human and divine love; the hopes and fears and the joys and sorrows that are the perdurable stuff of existence, the inexhaustible and unchanging principles of activity in man. Now it is only to the few that reduced to their simplest expression the 'eternal verities' are engaging and impressive. To touch the many they must be conveyed in human terms; they must be presented not as impersonal abstractions, not as matter for the higher intelligence and the higher emotions, but as living, breathing, individual facts, vivid with the circumstance of terrene life, quick with the thoughts and ambitions of the hour, full charged with familiar and neighbourly associations. All this with Dr. Hake is by no means inevitable. He loves to symbolise; he does not always care that the symbol shall be appropriate and plain. He prefers to work in allegory and emblem; but he does not always see that, however representative to himself, his emblems and his allegories may not be altogether representative to the world. His imagination is at once quaint and far-reaching—at once peculiar and ambitious; and it is often guilty of what is recondite and remote. In his best work—in *Old Souls*, for instance, and *Old Morality*—the quaintness is merely decorative: the essentials are sound and human enough to be of lasting interest and to have a capacity of common application. Elsewhere his imagery is apt to become strange and unaffecting, his fancy to work in curious and desolate ways, his message to sound abstruse and strange; and these effects too are deepened by the qualities and the merits of his style. It is peculiarly his own, but it is not always felicitous. There are times when it has the true epic touch—or at least as much of it as is possible in an age of detail and elaboration; there are times when it has a touch of the pathetic—when in homeliness of phrase and triviality of rhythm it is hardly to be surpassed; and there are times, as in *The Snake Charmer* when, as in certain pages in the work of Richard Wagner, it is so studiously laboured and so heavily charged with ornament and colour as to be almost pedantic in infelicity, almost repellent by sheer force of superfluous and elaborate suggestiveness. Last of all, in an epoch trained upon the passionate and subtle cadences of the Laureate and the large-moulded, ample, irresistible melodies of Mr. Swinburne, Dr. Hake chooses to deal in rhythms of the utmost naïveté and in metrical forms that are simplicity itself.

LANDOR

Anti-Landor.

To the many, Landor has always been more or less unapproachable, and has always seemed more or less shadowy and unreal. To begin with, he wrote for himself and a few others, and principally for himself. Then, he wrote waywardly and unequally as well as selfishly; he published pretty much at random; the bulk of his work is large; and the majority has passed him by for writers more accessible and work less freakish and more comprehensible. It is probable too that even among those who, inspired by natural temerity or the intemperate curiosity of the general reader, have essayed his conquest and set out upon what has been described as 'the Adventure of the Seven Volumes which are Seven Valleys of Dry Bones,' but few have returned victorious. Of course the Seven Volumes are a world. But (it is objected) the world is peculiar in pattern, abounding in antres vast and desarts idle, in gaps and precipices and 'manifest solutions of continuity,' and enveloped in an atmosphere which ordinary lungs find now too rare and now too dense and too anodyne. Moreover, it is peopled chiefly with abstractions: bearing noble and suggestive names but all surprisingly alike in stature and feature, all more or less incapable of sustained emotion and even of logical argument, all inordinately addicted to superb generalities and a kind of monumental skittishness, all expressing themselves in a style whose principal characteristic is a magnificent monotony, and all apparently the outcome of a theory that to be wayward is to be creative, that human interest is a matter of apophthegms and oracular sentences, and that axiomatic and dramatic are identical qualities and convertible terms. This is the opinion of those adventurers in whom defeat has generated a sense of injury and an instinct of antagonism. Others less fortunate still have found Landor a continent of dulness and futility—have come to consider the Seven Volumes as so many aggregations of tedium. Such experiences are one-sided and partial no doubt; and considered from a certain point of view they seem worthless enough. But they exist, and they are in some sort justified. Landor, when all is said, remains a writers' writer; and for my part I find it impossible not to feel a certain sympathy with them that hesitate to accept him for anything else.

His Drama.

Again, to some of us Lander's imagination is not only inferior in kind but poverty-stricken in degree; his creative faculty is limited by the reflection that its one achievement is Landor; his claim to consideration as a dramatic writer is negatived by the fact that, poignant as are the situations with which he loved to deal, he was apparently incapable of perceiving their capacities: inasmuch as he has failed completely and logically to develop a single one of them; inasmuch, too, as he has never once succeeded in conceiving, much less in picturing, such a train of conflicting emotions as any one of the complications from which he starts might be supposed to generate. To many there is nothing Greek about his dramatic work except the absence of stage directions; and to these that quality of 'Landorian abruptness' which seems to Mr. Sidney Colvin to excuse so many of its shortcomings is identical with a certain sort of what in men of lesser mould is called stupidity.

HOOD

How Much of Him?

Hood wrote much for bread, and he wrote much under pressure of all manner of difficulties—want of health and want of money, the hardship of exile and the bitterness of comparative failure; and not a little of what he produced is the merest journalism, here to-day and gone to-morrow. At his highest he is very high, but it was not given to him to enjoy the conditions under which great work is produced: he had neither peace of body nor health of mind, his life from first to last was a struggle with sickness and misfortune. How is it possible to maintain an interest in all he wrote, when two-thirds of it was produced with duns at the door and a nurse in the other room and the printer's-devil waiting in the hall? Of his admirable courage, his fine temper, his unfailing goodness of heart, his incorruptible honesty, it were hard to speak too highly; for one has but to read the story of his life to wonder that he should have written anything at all. At his happiest he had the gift of laughter; at his deepest and truest the more precious gift of tears. But for him there were innumerable hours when the best he could affect was the hireling's motley; when his fun and his pathos alike ran strained and thin; when the unique poet and wit became a mere comic rhymester. Is it just to his memory that it should be burdened with such a mass of what is already antiquated? But one answer is possible. The immortal part of Hood might be expressed into a single tiny volume.

Death's Jest-Book.

Thackeray preferred Hood's passion to his fun; and Thackeray knew. Hood had an abundance of a certain sort of wit, the wit of odd analogies, of remote yet familiar resemblances, of quaint conceits and humourous and unexpected quirks. He made not epigrams but jokes, sometimes purely intellectual but nearly always with the verbal quality as well. The wonderful jingle called *Miss Kilmansegg*—hard and cold and glittering as the gold that gleams in it—abounds in capital types of both. But for an example of both here is a stanza taken at random from the *Ode to the Great Unknown*:—

'Thou *Scottish Barmecide*, feeding the hunger
  Of curiosity with airy gammon;
    Thou mystery-monger,
  Dealing it out like middle cut of salmon
That people buy and can't make head or tail of it,'

and so forth, and so forth: the first a specimen of oddness of analogy—the joke intellectual; the second a jest in which the intellectual quality is complicated with the verbal. Of rarer merit are that conceit of the door which was shut with such a slam 'it sounded like a wooden d---n,' and that mad description of the demented mariner,—

'His head was *turned*, and so he *chewed*
His *pigtail* till he died,'—

which is a pun as unexpected and imaginative as any that exists, not excepting even Lamb's renowned achievement, the immortal 'I say, Porter, is that your own Hare or a Wig?' But as a punster Hood is merely unsurpassable. The simplest and the most complex, the wildest and the most obvious, the straightest and the most perverse, all puns came alike to him. The form was his natural method of expression. His prose extravaganzas—even to the delightful *Friend in Need*—are pretty well forgotten; his one novel is very hard to read; there is far less in *Up the Rhine* than in *Humphry Clinker* after all; we have been spoiled for *Lycus the Centaur* and *The Plea of the Midsummer Fairies* by the rich and passionate verse of the Laureate, the distinction, and the measure of Arnold, the sumptuous diction and the varied and enchanting music of *Atalanta* and *Hesperia* and *Erechtheus*. We care little for the old-fashioned whimsicality of the *Odes*, and little for such an inimitable farrago of vulgarisms, such a *reductio ad absurdum* of sentiment and style, as *The Lost Child*. But the best of Hood's puns are amusing after forty years. They are the classics of verbal extravagance, and they are a thousand times better known than *The Last Man*, though that is a work of genius, and almost as popular as the *Song of the Shirt*, the *Bridge of Sighs*, the *Dream of Eugene Aram* themselves. By an odd chance, too, the rhymes in which they are set have all a tragic theme. 'Tout ce qui touche à la mort,' says Champfleury, 'est d'une gaieté folle.' Hood found out that much for himself before Champfleury had begun to write. His most riotous ballads are ballads of death and the grave. Tim Turpin does murder and is hanged

>   'On Horsham drop, and none can say
>   He took a drop too much';

Ben Battle entwines a rope about his melancholy neck, and for the second time in life *enlists him in the line*; Young Ben expires of grief for the falsehood of Sally Brown: Lieutenant Luff drinks himself into his grave; John Day the amorous coachman,

>   'With back too broad to be conceived
>   By any narrow mind,'

pines to nothingness, and is found heels uppermost in his cruel mistress's water-butt. To Hood, with his grim imagination and his strange fantastic humour, death was meat and drink. It is as though he saw so much of the 'execrable Shape' that at last the pair grew friends, and grinned whenever they foregathered even in thought.

His Immortal Part.

Was Thackeray right, then, in resenting the waste of Hood's genius upon mere comicalities? I think he was; but only to a certain point. Hood was a true poet: but it was not until after years of proof and endeavour that he discovered the use to which his powers could best be put and the material on which they could best be employed. He worked hard and with but partial success at poetry all his life long. He passed his life in punning and making comic assaults on the Queen's English; but he was author all the while of *The Plea of the Midsummer Fairies*, the *Ode to Melancholy*, *Hero and Leander*, *Lycus the Centaur*, and a score and more of lovable and moving ballads; and he had won himself a name with two such capital examples of melodrama as *The Last Man* (1826) and *The Dream of Eugene Aram* (1829). But as a poet he profited little. The public preferred him as a buffoon; and not until his last years (and then anonymously) was he able to utter his highest word. All was made ready against his coming—the age, the subject, the public mind, the public capacity of emotion; and in *The Song of the Shirt* he approved himself a great singer. In the days of *Lycus the Centaur* and the *Midsummer Fairies* he could no more have written it than the public could have heeded had he written. But times were changed—Dickens had come, and the humanitarian epoch—and the great song went like fire. So, a year or two after, did *The Bridge of Sighs*. That, says Thackeray, 'was his Corunna, his Heights of Abraham—sickly, weak, wounded, he fell in the full blaze and fame of that great victory.' Could he have repeated it had he lived? Who knows? In both these irresistible appeals to the heart of man the material is of equal value and importance with the form; and in poetry such material is rare. A brace of such songs is possible to a poet; ten couples are not. It is Hood's immortality that he sang these two. Almost in the uttering they went the round of the world; and it is not too much to say of them that they will only pass with the language.

LEVER

How He Lived.

The story of Lever's life and adventures only wants telling to be as irresistibly attractive as Lorrequer's or O'Malley's own. Born in Dublin, of an English father and an Irish mother, he lived to be essentially cosmopolitan and a *viveur* of the first magnitude. At eight he was master of his schoolmaster—a gentleman given to flogging but not learned in Greek, and therefore a proper subject for a certain sort of blackmailing. He was not an industrious boy; but he was apt and ready with his tongue, he was an expert in fencing and the dance, he was good at improvising and telling stories, it is on record that he pleaded and won the cause of himself and certain of his schoolmates accused before a magistrate of riot and outrage. At college he found work for his high spirits in wild fun and the perpetration of practical jokes. He and his chum Ottiwell, the original of Frank Webber, behaved to their governors, teachers, and companions very much as Charles O'Malley and the redoubtable Frank behave to theirs. Lever was excellent at a street-ballad, and made and sang them in the rags of Rhoudlim, just as Frank Webber does; and he personated Cusack the surgeon to Cusack's class, just as Frank Webber personates the dean to *his* class. On the whole, indeed, he must have been as gamesome and volatile a nuisance as even Dublin has endured. On leaving college he took charge of an emigrant ship bound for Quebec. Arrived in Canada, he plunged into the backwoods, was affiliated to a tribe of Indians, and had to escape like Bagenal Daly at the risk of his life. Then he went to Germany, became a student at Göttingen under Blumenbach, was heart and soul a Bursch, and had the honour of seeing Goethe at Weimar. His diploma gained, he went to Clare to do battle with the cholera and gather materials for *Harry Lorrequer*. After this he was for some time dispensary doctor at Portstewart, where he met Prebendary Maxwell, the wild parson who wrote *Captain Blake*: so that here and now it is natural to find him leaping turf-carts and running away from his creditors. At Brussels, where he physicked the British Embassy and the British tourist, he knew all sorts of people—among them Commissioner Meade, the original of Major Monsoon, and Cardinal Pecci, the original of Leo xiii.—and saw all sorts of life, and ran into all sorts of extravagance: until of a sudden, he is back again in the capital, editing the *Dublin University Magazine*. Of course he was the maddest editor ever seen. For him cards, horses, and high living were not luxuries but necessaries of life; yet all the while he believed devoutly in medicine, and with his family indulged with freedom in the use of calomel and such agents. Presently he abandoned Ireland for the Continent. He took his horses with him, and astonished Europe with a four-in-hand of his own. Carlsruhe knew him well, as Belgium and the Rhine had known him. He only left the Reider Schloss at Bregenz to conquer Italy; and at Florence, Spezzia, and finally Trieste, he shone like himself.

What He Was.

He was a born *poseur*. His vanity made him one of the worst—the most excessive—of talkers; go where he would and do what he might, he was unhappy if the first place were another's. In all he did he was greedy to excel, and to excel incontestably. Like his own Bagenal Daly he would have taken the big jump with the reins in his mouth and his hands tied, 'just to show the English Lord-Lieutenant how an Irish gentleman rides.' He was all his life long confounding an English Lord-Lieutenant of some sort; for without display he would have pined away and died. At Templeogue he lived at the rate of £3,000 a year on an income of £1,200; at Brussels he kept open house on little or nothing for all the wandering grandees of Europe; at Florence they used to liken the cavalcade from his house to a procession from Franconi's; he found living in a castle and spending £10 a day on his horses the finest fun in the world. He existed but to bewilder and dazzle, and had he not been a brilliant and distinguished novelist he would have been a brilliant and distinguished something else. As he kept open house everywhere, as he was fond of every sort of luxury, as he loved not less to lend money to his intimates than to lose it to them at cards, and as he got but poor prices for his novels and was not well paid for his consular services, it is not easy to see how he managed to make ends meet.

How He Wrote.

Nor is it easy to see how he contrived to produce his novels. He was too passionately addicted to society and the enjoyment of life to spare an instant from them if he could help it; and the wonder is not that he should have written so well but that he should have written at all. Fortunately or the other thing, his books cost him no effort. He wrote or dictated at a gallop and, his copy once produced, had finished his work. He abhorred revision, and while keenly sensitive to blame and greedy of praise he ceased to care for his books as soon as they had left his desk. That he was not in scarce any sense an artist is but too clear. He never worked on a definite plan nor was at any pains to contrive a plot; he depended on the morning's impressions for the evening's task, and wrote *Con Cregan* under the immediate influence of a travelled Austrian, who used to talk to him every night ere he sat down to his story. But he was a wonderful improvisatore. He had imagination—(even romantic imagination: as the episode of Menelaus Crick in *Con Cregan* will show)—a keen, sure eye for character, incomparable facility in composition, an inexhaustible fund of shrewdness, whimsicality, high spirits, an admirable knack of dialogue; and as consul at Spezzia and at Trieste, as a fashionable practitioner at Brussels, as dispensary doctor on the wild Ulster coast, he was excellently placed for the kind of literature it was in him to produce. Writing at random and always under the spur of necessity, he managed to inform his work with extraordinary vitality and charm. His books were only made to sell, but it is like enough that they will also live, for they are yet well nigh as readable as at first, and Nina and Kate O'Donoghue—(for instance)—seem destined to go down to posterity as typical and representative. Had their author taken art seriously, and devoted all his energy to its practice, he could scarce have done more than this. Perhaps, indeed, he would not have done so much. It could never have been Lorrequer's to 'build the lofty rhyme.' It was an honest as well as a brilliant creature; and I believe we should all have suffered if some avenging chance had borne it in upon him that to be really lofty your rhyme must of necessity be not blown upwards like a bubble but built in air like a cathedral. He would, I take it, have experimentalised in repentance to the extent of elaborating his creations and chastising his style; and, it may be, he would have contrived but to beggar his work of interest and correct himself of charm. A respectable ambition, no doubt; but how much better to be the rough-and-ready artist of Darby the Beast and Micky Free, the humane and charming rattlepate to whom we owe Paul Goslett and the excellent and pleasing Potts!

JEFFERIES

His Virtue.

I love to think of Jefferies as a kind of literary Leatherstocking. His style, his mental qualities, the field he worked in, the chase he followed, were peculiar to himself, and as he was without a rival, so was he without a second. Reduced to its simplest expression, his was a mind compact of observation and of memory. He writes as one who watches always, who sees everything, who forgets nothing. As his lot was cast in country places, among wood and pasturage and corn, by coverts teeming with game and quick with insect life, and as withal he had the hunter's patience and quick-sightedness, his faculty of looking and listening and of noting and remembering, his readiness of deduction and insistence of pursuit—there entered gradually into his mind a greater quantity of natural England, her leaves and flowers, her winds and skies, her wild things and tame, her beauties and humours and discomforts, than was ever, perhaps, the possession of writing Briton. This property he conveyed to his countrymen in a series of books of singular freshness and interest. The style is too formal and sober, the English seldom other than homely and sufficient; there is overmuch of the reporter and nothing like enough of the artist, the note of imagination, the right creative faculty. But they are remarkable books. It is not safe to try and be beforehand with posterity, but in the case of such works as the *Gamekeeper* and *Wild Life* and with such a precedent as that established by the *Natural History of Selborne* such anticipation seems more tempting and less hazardous than usual. One has only to think of some mediæval Jefferies attached to the staff of Robin Hood, and writing about Needwood and Charnwood as his descendant wrote about the South Downs, to imagine an historical document of priceless value and inexhaustible interest. And in years to be, when the whole island is one vast congeries of streets, and the fox has gone down to the bustard and the dodo, and outside museums of comparative anatomy the weasel is not and the badger has ceased from the face of the earth, it is not doubtful that the *Gamekeeper* and *Wild Life* and the *Poacher*—epitomising, as they will, the rural England of certain centuries before—will be serving as material and authority for historical descriptions, historical novels, historical epics, historical pictures, and will be honoured as the most useful stuff of their kind in being.

His Limitation.

In those first books of his Jefferies compels attention by sheer freshness of matter; he is brimful of new facts and original and pertinent observation, and that every one is vaguely familiar with and interested in the objects he is handling and explaining serves but to heighten his attractiveness. There are so many who but know of hares disguised as soup, of ants as a people on whose houses it is not good to sit down, of partridges as a motive of bread sauce! And Jefferies, retailing in plain, useful English the thousand and one curious facts that make up life for these creatures and their kind—Jefferies walking the wood, or tracking the brook, or mapping out the big tree—is some one to be heeded with gratitude. He is the Scandalous Chronicler of the warren and the rookery, the newsmonger and intelligencer of creeping things, and things that fly, and things that run; and his confidences, unique in quality and type, have the novelty and force of personal revelations. In dealing with men and women, he surrendered most of his advantage and lost the best part of his charm. The theme is old, the matter well worn, the subject common to us all; and most of us care nothing for a few facts more or less unless they be romantically conveyed. Reality is but the beginning, the raw material, of art; and it is by the artist's aid and countenance that we are used to make acquaintance with our fellows, be they generals in cocked hats or mechanics in fustian. Now Jefferies was not an artist, and so beside his stoats and hares, his pike, his rabbits, and his moles, his men and women are of little moment. You seem to have heard of them and to far better purpose from others; you have had their author's facts presented elsewhere, and that in picturesque conjunction with the great eternal interests of passion and emotion. To be aware of such a difference is to resent it; and accordingly to read is to know that Jefferies would have done well to leave Hodge and Hodge's masters alone and keep to his beasts and birds and fishes.

The General.

Is it not plain as the nose on your face that his admirers admire him injudiciously? It is true, for instance, that he is in a sense, 'too full' (the phrase is Mr. Besant's) for the generality of readers. But it is also true that he is not nearly full enough: that they look for conclusions while he is bent upon giving them only details: that they clamour for a breath of inspiration while he is bent upon emptying his note-book in decent English; that they persist in demanding a motive, a leading idea, a justification, while he with knowledge crammed is fixed in his resolve to tell them no more than that there are milestones on the Dover Road, or that there are so many nails of so many shapes and so many colours in the pig-sty at the back of Coate Farm. They prefer 'their geraniums in the conservatory.' They refuse, in any case, to call a 'picture' that which is only a long-drawn sequence of statements. They are naturally inartistic, but they have the tradition of a long and speaking series of artistic results, and instinctively they decline to recognise as art the work of one who was plainly the reverse of an artist. The artist is he who knows how to select and to inspire the results of his selection. Jefferies could do neither. He was a reporter of genius; and he never got beyond reporting. To the average reader he is wanting in the great essentials of excitement: he is prodigal of facts, and he contrives to set none down so as to make one believe in it for longer than the instant of perusal. From his work the passionate human quality is not less absent than the capacity of selection and the gift of inspiration, and all the enthusiasm of all the enthusiasts of an enthusiastic age will not make him and his work acceptable to the aforesaid average reader. In letters he is as the ideal British water-colourist in paint: the care of both is not art but facts, and again facts, and facts ever. You consider their work; you cannot see the wood for the trees; and you are fain to conclude that themselves were so much interested in the trees they did not even know the wood was there.

Last Words.

To come to an end with the man:—his range was very limited, and within that range his activity was excessive; yet the consequences of his enormous effort were—and are—a trifle disappointing. He thought, poor fellow! that he had the world in his hand and the public at his feet; whereas, the truth to tell, he had only the empire of a kind of back garden and the lordship of (as Mr. Besant has told us) some forty thousand out of a hundred millions of readers. You know that he suffered greatly; you know too that to the last he worked and battled on as became an honest, much-enduring, self-admiring man: as you know that in death he snatched a kind of victory, and departed this life with dignity as one 'good at many things,' who had at last 'attained to be at rest.' You know, in a word, that he took his part in the general struggle for existence, and manfully did his best; and it is with something like a pang that you find his biographer insisting on the merits of the feat, and quoting approvingly the sentimentalists who gathered about his death-bed. To make eloquence about heroism is not the way to breed heroes; and it may be that Jefferies, had his last environment been less fluent and sonorous, would now seem something more heroic than he does.

GAY

The Fabulist.

Gay the fabulist is only interesting in a certain sense and to a small extent. The morality of the *Fables* is commonplace; their workmanship is only facile and agreeable; as literature—as achievements in a certain order of art—they have a poor enough kind of existence. In comparison to the work of La Fontaine they are the merest journalism. The simplicity, the wit, the wisdom, the humanity, the dramatic imagination, the capacity of dramatic expression, the exquisite union of sense and manner, the faultless balance of matter and style, are qualities for which in the Englishman you look in vain. You read, and you read not only without enthusiasm but without interest. The verse is merely brisk and fluent; the invention is common; the wit is not very witty; the humour is artificial; the wisdom, the morality, the knowledge of life, the science of character—if they exist at all it is but as anatomical preparations or plants in a *hortus siccus*. Worse than anything, the *Fables* are monotonous. The manner is consistently uniform; the invention has the level sameness of a Lincolnshire landscape; the narrative moves with the equal pace of boats on a Dutch canal. The effect is that of a host of flower-pots, the columns in a ledger, a tragedy by the Rev.

Mr. Home; and it is heightened by the matchless triteness of the fabulist's reflections and the uncommon tameness of his drama. It is hard to believe that this is indeed the Gay of *Polly* and *The Beggars' Opera*. True, the dialects of his Peachum and his Lockit are in some sort one; his gentlemen of the road and his ladies of the kennel rejoice in a common flippancy of expression; there is little to choose between the speech of Polly and the speech of Lucy. But in respect of the essentials of drama the dialogue of the *Beggars' Opera* is on the whole sufficient. The personages are puppets; but they are individual, and they are fairly consistent in their individuality. Miss Lockit does not think and feel like Miss Diver; Macheath is distinguishable from Peachum; none is exactly alive, but of stage life ail have their share. The reverse of this is the case with the personages of the *Fables*. They think the thoughts and speak the speech of Mr. Gay. The elephant has the voice of the sparrow; the monkey is one with the organ on which he sits; there is but a difference of name between the eagle and the hog; the talk of Death has exactly the manner and weight and cadence of the Woodman's; a change of label would enable the lion to change places with the spaniel, would suffice to cage the wolf as a bird and set free the parrot as a beast of prey. All are equally pert, brisk, and dapper in expression; all are equally sententious and smart in aim; all are absolutely identical in function and effect. The whole gathering is stuffed with the same straw, prepared with the same dressing, ticketed in the same handwriting, and painted with the same colours. Any one who remembers the infinite variety of La Fontaine will feel that Gay the fabulist is a writer whose work the world has let die very willingly indeed.

The Moralist.

And Gay is not a whit less inefficient as a moralist. He is a kindly soul, and in his easygoing way he has learnt something of the tricks of the world and something of the hearts of men. He writes as an unsuccessful courtier; and in that capacity he has remarks to offer which are not always valueless, and in which there is sometimes a certain shrewdness. But the unsuccessful courtier is on the whole a creature of the past. Such interest as he has is rather historical than actual; and neither in the nursery nor in the schoolroom is he likely to create any excitement or be received with any enthusiasm. To the world he can only recommend himself as one anxious to make it known on the smallest provocation and on any occasion or none that Queen Anne is dead. Open him where you will, and you find him full of this important news and determined on imparting it. Thus, in *The Scold and the Parrot*:

'One slander must ten thousand get,
The world with int'rest pays the debt';

that is to say, Queen Anne is dead. Thus, too, in *The Persian, the Sun, and the Cloud*:

'The gale arose; the vapour tost
(The sport of winds) in air was lost;
The glorious orb the day refines.
Thus envy breaks, thus merit shines';

in *The Goat without a Beard*:

'Coxcombs distinguished from the rest
To all but coxcombs are a jest';

in *The Shepherd's Dog and the Wolf*:

'An open foe may prove a curse,
But a pretended friend is worse';

and so to the end of the chapter. The theme is not absorbing, and the variations are proper to the theme.

After All.

How long is it that the wise and good have ceased to say (striking their pensive bosoms), '*Here* lies Gay'? It is—how long? But for all that Gay is yet a figure in English letters. As a song-writer he has still a claim on us, and is still able to touch the heart and charm the ear. The lyrics in *Acis and Galatea* are not unworthy their association with Handel's immortal melodies, the songs in *The Beggars' Opera* have a part in the life and fame of the sweet old tunes from which they can never be divided. I like to believe that in the operas and the *Trivia* and *The Shepherd's Week* is buried the material of a pleasant little book.

ESSAYS AND ESSAYISTS

The Good of Them.

It is our misfortune that of good essayists there should be but few. Men there have been who have done the essayist's part so well as to have earned an immortality in the doing; but we have had not many of them, and they make but a poor figure on our shelves. It is a pity that things should be thus with us, for a good essayist is the pleasantest companion imaginable. There are folk in plenty who have never read Montaigne at all; but there are few indeed who have read but a page of him, and that page but once. And the same may be said of Addison and Fielding, of Lamb and Hazlitt, of Sterne and Bacon and Ben Jonson, and all the members of their goodly fellowship. To sit down with any one of them is to sit down in the company of one of the 'mighty wits, our elders and our betters,' who have done much to make literature a good thing, having written books that are eternally readable. If of all them that have tried to write essays and succeeded after a fashion a twentieth part so much could be said the world would have a conversational literature of inexhaustible interest. But indeed there is nothing of the sort. Beside the 'rare and radiant' masters of the art there are the apprentices, and these are many and dull.

Generalities.

Essayists, like poets, are born and not made, and for one worth remembering the world is confronted with a hundred not worth reading. Your true essayist is in a literary sense the friend of everybody. As one of the brotherhood has phrased it, it is his function 'to speak with ease and opportunity to all men.' He must be personal, or his hearers can feel no manner of interest in him. He must be candid and sincere, or his readers presently see through him. He must have learned to think for himself and to consider his surroundings with an eye that is both kindly and observant, or they straightway find his company unprofitable. He should have fancy, or his starveling propositions will perish for lack of metaphor and the tropes and figures needed to vitalise a truism. He does well to have humour, for humour makes men brothers, and is perhaps more influential in an essay than in most places else. He will find a little wit both serviceable to himself and comfortable to his readers. For wisdom, it is not absolutely necessary that he have it, but in its way it is as good a property as any: used with judgment, indeed, it does more to keep an essay sweet and fresh than almost any other quality. And in default of wisdom—which, to be sure, it is not given to every man, much less to every essayist, to entertain—he need have no scruples about using whatever common sense is his; for common sense is a highly respectable commodity, and never fails of a wide and eager circle of buyers. A knowledge of men and of books is also to be desired; for it is a writer's best reason of being, and without it he does well to hold his tongue. Blessed with these attributes he is an essayist to some purpose. Give him leisure and occasion, and his discourse may well become as popular as Montaigne's own.

In Particular.

For the British essayists, they are more talked about than known. It is to be suspected that from the first their reputation has greatly exceeded their popularity; and of late years, in spite of the declamation of Macaulay and the very literary enthusiasm of the artist of *Esmond* and *The Virginians*, they have fallen further into the background, and are less than ever studied with regard. In theory the age of Anne is still the Augustan age to us; but in theory only, and only to a certain extent. What attracts us is its outside. We are in love with its houses and its china and its costumes. We are not enamoured of it as it was but as it seems to Mr. Caldecott and Mr. Dobson and Miss Kate Greenaway. We care little for its comedy and nothing at all for its tragedy. Its verse is all that our own is not, and the same may be said of its prose and ours—of the prose of Mr. Swinburne and Mr. George Meredith and the prose of Addison and Swift. Mr.

Gladstone is not a bit like Bolingbroke, and between *The Times* and *The Tatler*, between *The Spectator* (Mr. Addison's), and *The Fortnightly Review*, there is a difference of close upon two centuries and of a dozen revolutions—political, social, scientific, and æsthetic. We may babble as we please about the 'sweetness' of Steele and the 'humour' of Sir Roger de Coverley, but in our hearts we care for them a great deal less than we ought, and in fact Mr. Mudie's subscribers do not hesitate to prefer the 'sweetness' of Mr. Black and the 'humour' of Mr. James Payn. Our love is not for the essentials of the time but only its accidents and oddities; and we express it in pictures and poems and fantasies in architecture, and the canonisation (in figures) of Chippendale and Sheraton. But it is questionable if we might not with advantage increase our interest, and carry imitation a little deeper. The Essayists, for instance, are often dull, but they write like scholars and gentlemen. They refrain from personalities; they let scandal alone, nor ever condescend to eavesdropping; they never go out of their way in search of affectation or prurience or melancholy, but are content to be merely wise and cheerful and humane. Above all, they do their work as well as they can. They seem to write not for bread nor for a place in society but for the pleasure of writing, and of writing well. In these hysterical times life is so full, so much is asked and so much has to be given, that tranquil writing and careful workmanship are impossible. A certain poet has bewailed the change in a charming rondeau:—

'More swiftly now the hours take flight!
What's read at morn is dead at night;
Scant space have we for art's delays,
Whose breathless thought so briefly stays,
We may not work—ah! would we might,
　　With slower pen!'

It must be owned that his melancholy is anything but groundless. The trick of amenity and good breeding is lost; the graces of an excellence that is unobtrusive are graces no more. We write as men paint for the exhibitions: with the consciousness that we must pass without notice if we do not exceed in colour and subject and tone. The need exists, and the world bows to it. Mr. Austin Dobson's little sheaf of *Eighteenth Century Essays* might be regarded as a protest against the necessity and the submission. It proves that 'tis possible to be eloquent without adjectives and elegant without affectation; that to be brilliant you need not necessarily be extravagant and conceited; that without being maudlin and sentimental it is not beyond mortal capacity to be pathetic; and that once upon a time a writer could prove himself a humourist without feeling it incumbent upon him to be also a jack-pudding.

BOSWELL

His Destiny.

It has been Boswell's fate to be universally read and almost as universally despised. What he suffered at the hands of Croker and Macaulay is typical of his fortune. In character, in politics, in attainments, in capacity, the two were poles apart; but they were agreed in this: that Boswell must be castigated and contemned, and that they were the men to do it. Croker's achievement, consider it how you will, remains the most preposterous in literary history. He could see nothing in the *Life* but a highly entertaining compilation greatly in need of annotation and correction. Accordingly he took up Boswell's text and interlarded it with scraps of his own and other people's; he pegged into it a sophisticated version of the *Tour*; and he overwhelmed his amazing compound with notes and commentaries in which he took occasion to snub, scold, 'improve,' and insult his author at every turn. What came of it one knows. Macaulay, in the combined interests of Whiggism and good literature, made Boswell's quarrel his own, and the expiation was as bitter as the offence was wanton and scandalous.

His Critic.

But Macaulay, if he did Jeddart justice on Croker, took care not to forget that Johnson was a Tory hero, and that Boswell was Johnson's biographer. He was too fond of good reading not to esteem the *Life* for one of the best of books. But he was also a master of the art of brilliant and picturesque misrepresentation; and he did not neglect to prove that the *Life* is only admirable because Boswell was contemptible. It was, he argued, only by virtue of being at once daft and drunken, selfish and silly, an eavesdropper and a talebearer, a kind of inspired Faddle, a combination of butt and lackey and snob, that Boswell contrived to achieve his wretched immortality. And in the same way Boswell's hero was after all but a sort of Grub Street Cyclops, respectable enough by his intelligence—(but even so ridiculous in comparison to gifted Whigs)—yet more or less despicable in his manners, his English, and his politics. Now, Macaulay was the genius of special pleading. Admirable man of letters as he was, he was politician first and man of letters afterwards: his judgments are no more final than his antitheses are dull, and his method for all its brilliance is the reverse of sound. When you begin to inquire how much he really knew about Boswell, and how far you may accept his own estimate of his own pretentions, he becomes amusing in spite of himself: much as, according to him, Boswell was an artist. In his review of Croker he is keen enough about dates and facts and solecisms; on questions of this sort he bestows his fiercest energies; for such lapses he visits his Tory opposite with his most savage and splendid insolence, his heartiest contempt, his most scathing rhetoric. But on the great question of all—the corruption of Boswell's text—he is not nearly so implacable, and concerning the foisting on the *Life* of the whole bulk of the *Tour* he is not more than lukewarm. 'We greatly doubt,' he says, 'whether *even* the *Tour to the Hebrides* should have been inserted in the midst of the *Life*. There is one marked distinction between the two works. Most of the *Tour* was seen by Johnson in manuscript. It does not appear that he ever saw any part of the *Life*.' This is to say that Croker's action is reprehensible not because it is an offence against art but because Johnson on private and personal grounds might not have been disposed to accept the *Life* as representative and just, and might have refused to sanction its appearance on an equal footing with the *Tour*, which on private and personal grounds he *had* accepted. In the face of such an argument who can help suspecting Macaulay's artistic faculty? 'The *Life of Johnson*,' he says, 'is assuredly a great, a very great, book. Homer is not more decidedly the first of heroic poets, Shakespeare is not more decidedly the first of dramatists, Demosthenes is not more decidedly the first of orators, than Boswell is the first of biographers . . . Eclipse is first, and the rest nowhere.' That is hearty and exact enough. But, as I have hinted, Macaulay, furious with Croker's carelessness, is almost tolerant of Croker's impudence. For Croker as a scholar and an historian he is merely pitiless; to Croker ruining the *Life* by the insertion of the *Tour*—a feat which would scarce be surpassed by the interpolation of the Falstaff scenes of the *Merry Wives* in one or other of the parts of *Henry IV.*—he is lenient enough, and lenient on grounds which are not artistic but purely moral. Did he recognise to the full the fact of Boswell's pre-eminence as an artist? Was he really conscious that the *Life* is an admirable work of art as well as the most readable and companionable of books? As, not content with committing himself thus far, he goes on to prove that Boswell was great because he was little, that he wrote a great book because he was an ass, and that if he had not been an ass his book would probably have been at least a small one, incredulity on these points becomes respectable.

Himself.

Boswell knew better. A true Scotsman and a true artist, he could play the fool on occasion, and he could profit by his folly. In his dedication to the first and greatest President the Royal Academy has had he anticipates a good many of Macaulay's objections to his character and deportment, and proves conclusively that if he chose to seem ridiculous he did so not unwittingly but with a complete apprehension of the effect he designed and the means he adopted. In the *Tour*, says he, from his 'eagerness to display the wonderful fertility and readiness of Johnson's wit,' he 'freely showed to the world its dexterity, even when I was myself the object of it.' He was under the impression that he would be 'liberally understood,' as 'knowing very well what I was about.' But, he adds, 'it seems I judged too well of the world'; and he points his moral with a story of 'the great Dr. Clarke,' who, 'unbending himself with a few friends in the most playful and frolicsome manner,' saw Beau Nash in the distance, and was instantly sobered. 'My boys,' quoth he, 'let us be grave—here comes a fool.' Macaulay was not exactly Beau Nash, nor was Boswell 'the great Dr. Clarke'; but, as Macaulay, working on Wolcot's lines, was presently to show, Boswell did right to describe the world as 'a great fool,' and to regret in respect of his own silliness that in the *Tour* he had been 'arrogant enough to suppose that the tenour of the rest of the book would sufficiently guard against such a strange imputation.' In the same way he showed himself fully alive to the enduring merits of his achievement. 'I will venture to say,' he writes, 'that he (Johnson) will be seen in this work more completely than any man who has ever lived.' He had his own idea of biography; he had demonstrated its value triumphantly in the *Tour* which, though organically complete, is plainly not a record of travel but a biographical essay. In the *Tour*, that is, he had approved himself an original master of selection, composition, and design; of the art of working a large number of essential details into a uniform and living whole; and of that most difficult and telling of accomplishments, the reproduction of talk. In the *Life* he repeated the proof on a larger scale and with a finer mastery of construction and effect; and in what his best editor describes as 'the task of correcting, amending, and adding to his darling work' he spent his few remaining years. That he drifted into greatness, produced his two masterpieces unconsciously, and developed a genius for biography as one develops a disease, is 'a ridiculous conception,' as Mr. Napier rightly says. In proof of it we have Boswell's own words, and we have the books themselves. Such testimony is not to be overborne by any number of paradoxes, however ingenious, nor by any superflux of rhetoric, however plausible and persuasive. That Boswell was a gossip, a busybody, and something of a sot, and that many did and still do call him fool, is certain; but that is no reason why he should not have been an artist, and none why he should be credited with the fame of having devoted the best part of his life to the production of a couple of masterpieces—as M. Jourdain talked prose—without knowing what he was doing. Turner chose to go a-masquerading as 'Puggy Booth'; but as yet nobody has put forward the assertion that Turner was unconscious of the romance and splendour of his *Ulysses and Polyphemus*, or that he painted his *Rain, Speed, and Steam* in absolute ignorance of the impression it would produce and the idea it should convey. Goldsmith reminded Miss Reynolds of 'a low mechanic, particularly . . . a journey-man tailor'; but that he was unconsciously the most elegant and natural writer of his age is a position which has not yet been advanced. And surely it is high time that Boswell should take that place in art which is his by right of conquest, and that Macaulay's paradox—which is only the opinion brilliantly put of an ignorant and unthinking world—('Il avait mieux que personne l'esprit de tout le monde')—should go the way of all its kind.

CONGREVE

His Biographers and Critics.

An American literary journal once assured its readers that Congreve has a 'niche in the Valhalla of Ben Jonson.' The remark is injudicious, of course, even for a literary American, and there is no apparent reason why it should ever have got itself uttered. It is probably the unluckiest thing that ever was said of Congreve, who—with some unimportant exceptions—has been singularly fortunate in his critics and biographers. Dryden wrote of him with enthusiasm, and in doing so he may be said to have set a fashion of admiration which is vigorous and captivating even yet. Swift, Voltaire, Lamb, Hunt, Hazlitt, Thackeray, Macaulay, to name but these, have dealt with him in their several ways; of late he has been praised by such masters of the art of writing as Mr. Swinburne and Mr. George Meredith; while Mr. Gosse, the last on the list, surpasses most of his predecessors in admiration and nearly all, I think, in knowledge.

The Real Congreve.

It is no fault of Mr. Gosse's that with all his diligence he should fail to give a complete and striking portrait of his man, or to make more of what he describes as his 'smiling, faultless rotundity.' As he puts it: 'There were no salient points about Congreve's character,' so that 'no vagaries, no escapades place him in a ludicrous or in a human light,' and 'he passes through the literary life of his time as if in felt slippers, noiseless, unupbraiding, without personal adventures.' That, I take it, is absolutely true. It is known that Congreve was cheerful, serviceable, and witty; that he was a man of many friends; that Pope dedicated his *Iliad* to him; that Dryden loved and admired him; that Collier attacked his work, and that his rejoinder was equally spiritless and ill-bred; that he was attached to Mrs. Bracegirdle, and left all his money to the Duchess of Marlborough; that he was a creditable Government official; and that at thirty, having written a certain number of plays, he suddenly lost his interest in life and art, and wrote no more. But that is about all. Thackeray's picture of him may be, and probably is, as unveracious as his Fielding or his Dick Steele; but there is little or nothing to show how far we can depend upon it. The character of the man escapes us, and we have either to refrain from trying to see him or to content ourselves with mere hypothesis. So abnormal is the mystery in which he is enshrouded that what in the case of others would be notorious remains in his case dubious and obscure: so that we cannot tell whether he was Bracegirdle's lover or only her friend, and the secret of his relations with the Duchess of Marlborough has yet to be discovered. Mr. Gosse succeeded no better than they that went before in plucking out the heart of Congreve's mystery. He was, and he remains, impersonal. At his most substantial he is (as some one said of him) no more than 'vagueness personified': at his most luminous only an appearance like the *Scin-Laeca*, the shining shadow adapted in a moment of peculiar inspiration by the late Lord Lytton.

The Dramatist.

But we have the plays, and who runs may read and admire. I say advisedly who runs may read, and not who will may see. Congreve's plays are, one can imagine, as dull in action as they are entertaining in print. They have dropped out of the *répertoire*, and the truth is they merit no better fate. They are only plays to the critic of style; to the actor and the average spectator they are merely so much spoken weariness. To begin with, they are marked by such a deliberate and immitigable baseness of morality as makes them impossible to man. Wycherley has done more vilely; Vanbrugh soars to loftier altitudes of filthiness. But neither Wycherley nor Vanbrugh has any strain of the admirable intellectual quality of Congreve. Villainy comes natural to the one, and beastliness drops from the other as easily as honey from the comb; but in neither is there evident that admirable effort of the intelligence which is a distinguishing characteristic of Congreve, and with neither is the result at once so consummate and so tame. For both Wycherley and Vanbrugh are playwrights, and Congreve is not. Congreve is only an artist in style writing for himself and half a dozen in the pit, while Wycherley and Vanbrugh—and for that matter Etherege and Farquhar—are playwrights producing for the whole theatre. In fact Congreve's plays were only successful in proportion as they were less literary and 'Congrevean.' His first comedy was the talk of the town; his last, *The Way of the World*, that monument of characterisation (of a kind) and fine English, was only a 'success of esteem.' The reason is not far to seek. Congreve's plays were too sordid in conception and too unamusing in effect for even the audiences to which they were produced; they were excellent literature, but they were bad drama, and they were innately detestable to boot. Audiences are the same in all strata of time; and it is easy to see that Wycherley's Horner and Vanbrugh's Sir John and Lady Brute were amusing, when Lady Wishfort and Sir Sampson Legend and the illustrious and impossible Maskwell were found 'old, cold, withered, and of intolerable entrails.' An audience, whatever its epoch, wants action; and still action, and again and for the last time action; also it wants a point of departure that shall be something tinctured with humanity, a touch of the human in the term of everything, and at least a 'sort of a kind of a strain' of humanity in the progress of events from the one point to the other. This it gets in

Wycherley, brute as he is; with a far larger and more vigorous comic sense it gets the same in Vanbrugh; it gets it with a difference in the light-hearted indecencies of Farquhar. From the magnificent prose of Congreve it is absent. His it was to sublimate all that was most artificial in an artificial state of society: he was the consummate artist of a phase that was merely transient, the laureate of a generation that was only alive for half-an-hour in the course of all the twenty-four. He is saved from oblivion by sheer strength of style. It is a bad dramatic style, as we know; it leaves the Witwoulds and the Plyants as admirable as the Mirabels and Millamants and Angelicas; it makes no distinction between the Mrs. Foresights and the Sir Sampson Legends; it presents an exemplar in Lady Wishfort and an exemplar in Petulant; it is uneasy, self-conscious, intrusive, even offensive, the very reverse of dramatic; and in Congreve's hands it is irresistible, for, thanks to Congreve, it has been forced from the stage, and lives as literature alone.

The Writer.

Congreve was essentially a man of letters; his style is that of a pupil not of Molière but of the full, the rich, the excessive, the pedantic Jonson; his Legends, his Wishforts, his Foresights are the lawful heirs—refined and sublimated but still of direct descent—of the Tuccas and the Bobadils and the Epicure Mammons of the great Elizabethan; they are (that is) more literary than theatrical—they are excellent reading, but they have long since fled the stage and vanished into the night of mere scholarship. To compare an author of this type and descent to Shakespeare is a trifle unfair; to compare him to Molière is to misapprehend the differences between pure literature and literature that is also drama. Congreve, as I have said, has disappeared from the boards, and is only tolerable or even intelligible to the true reader; while Shakespeare worked on so imperfect a convention that, though he keeps the stage and is known indeed for the poet of the most popular play ever written—(for that, I take it, *Hamlet* is)—he is yet the prey of every twopenny actor, or actor-manager, or actor-manager-editor, who is driven to deal with him. Now, Molière wrote as one that was first of all a great actor; who dealt not so much with what is transient in human life as with what is eternal in human nature; who addressed himself much more to an audience—(Fénelon who found fault with his style is witness to the fact)—than to a circle of readers. And the result is that Molière not only remains better reading than Congreve, but is played at this time in the Rue de Richelieu line for line and word for word as he was played at the Palais-Bourbon over two hundred years ago.

ARABIAN NIGHTS ENTERTAINMENTS

Its Romance.

He that has the book of the *Thousand Nights and a Night* has Hachisch-made-words for life. Gallant, subtle, refined, intense, humourous, obscene, here is the Arab intelligence drunk with conception. It is a vast extravaganza of passion in action and picarooning farce and material splendour run mad. The amorous instinct and the instinct of enjoyment, not tempered but heightened greatly by the strict ordinances of dogma, have leave to riot uncontrolled. It is the old immortal story of Youth and Beauty and their coming together, but it is coloured with the hard and brilliant hues of an imagination as sensuous in type and as gorgeous in ambition as humanity has known. The lovers must suffer, for suffering intensifies the joy of fruition; so they are subjected to all such modes of travail and estrangement as a fancy careless of pain and indifferent to life can devise. But it is known that happy they are to be; and if by the annihilation of time and space then are space and time annihilated. Adventures are to the adventurous all the world over; but they are so with a difference in the East. It is only Sinbad that confesses himself devoured with the lust of travel. The grip of a humourous and fantastic fate is tight on all the other heroes of this epic-in-bits. They do not go questing for accidents: their hour comes, and the finger of God urges them forth, and thrusts them on in the way of destiny. The air is horrible with the gross and passionate figments of Islamite mythology. Afrits watch over or molest them; they are made captive of malignant Ghouls; the Jinns take bodily form and woo them to their embraces. The sea-horse ramps at them from the ocean floor; the great roc darkens earth about them with the shadow of his wings; wise and goodly apes come forth and minister unto them; enchanted camels bear them over evil deserts with the swiftness of the wind, or the magic horse outspreads his sail-broad vannes, and soars with them; or they are borne aloft by some servant of the Spell till the earth is as a bowl beneath them, and they hear the angels quiring at the foot of the Throne. So they fare to strange and dismal places: through cities of brass whose millions have perished by divine decree; cities guilty of the cult of the Fire and the Light wherein all life has been striken to stone; or on to the magnetic mountain by whose horrible attraction the bolts are drawn from the ship, and they alone survive the inevitable wreck. And the end comes. Comes the Castle of Burnished Copper, and its gates fly open before them: the forty damsels, each one fairer than the rest, troop out at their approach; they are bathed in odours, clothed in glittering apparel, fed with enchanted meats, plunged fathoms deep in the delights of the flesh. There is contrived for them a private paradise of luxury and splendour, a practical Infinite of gold and silver stuffs and jewels and all things gorgeous and rare and costly; and therein do they abide for evermore. You would say of their poets that they contract immensity to the limits of desire; they exhaust the inexhaustible in their enormous effort; they stoop the universe to the slavery of a talisman, and bind the visible and invisible worlds within the compass of a ring.

Its Comedy.

But there is another side to their imaginings. When the Magian has done beating his copper drum—(how its mysterious murmur still haunts the echoes of memory!)—when Queen Lab has finished her tremendous conjurations, wonder gives place to laughter, the apotheosis of the flesh to the spirit of comedy. The enchanter turns harlequin; and what the lovers ask is not the annihilation of time and space but only that the father be at his prayers, or the husband gone on a fool's errand, while they have leave to kiss each other's mouths, 'as a pigeon feedeth her young,' to touch the lute, strip language naked, and 'repeat the following verses' to a ring of laughing girls and amid all such comfits and delicates as a hungry audience may rejoice to hear enumerated. And the intrigue begins, and therewith the presentment of character, the portraiture of manners. Merry ladies make love to their gallants with flowers, or scorn them with the huckle-bones of shame; the Mother Coles of Araby pursue the unwary stranger for their mistress' pleasure; damsels resembling the full moon carouse with genial merchants or inquiring calenders. The beast of burden, even the porter, has his hour: he goes the round at the heels of a veiled but beautiful lady, and lays her in the materials of as liberal and sumptuous a carouse as is recorded in history. Happy lady, and O thrice-fortunate porter! enviable even to the term of time! It is a voluptuous farce, a masque and anti-masque of wantonness and stratagem, of wine-cups and jewels and fine raiment, of gaudy nights and amorous days, of careless husbands and adventurous wives, of innocent fathers and rebel daughters and lovers happy or befooled. And high over all, his heart contracted with the spleen of the East, the tedium of supremacy, towers the great Caliph Haroun, the buxom and bloody tyrant, a Muslim Lord of Misrule. With Giafar, the finest gentleman and goodliest gallant of Eastern story, and Mesrour, the well-beloved, the immortal Eunuch, he goes forth upon his round in the enchanted streets of Bagdàd, like François Premier in the maze of old-time Paris. The night is musical with happy laughter and the sound of lutes and voices; it is seductive with the clink of goblets and the odour of perfumes: not a shadow but has its secret, or jovial or amorous or terrible: here falls a head, and there you may note the contrapuntal effect of the bastinado. But the blood is quickly hidden with flowers, the bruises are tired over with cloth-of-gold, and the jolly pageant sweeps on. Truly the comic essence is imperishable. What was fun to them in Baghdad is fun to us in London after a thousand years.

Sacer Vates.

The prose of Mr. Payne's translation is always readable and often elegant; Sir Richard Burton's notes and 'terminal essays' are a mine of curious and diverting information; but for me the real author of *The Arabian Nights* is called not Burton nor Payne but Antoine Galland. He it was, in truth, who gave the world as much exactly as it needed of his preposterous original: who eliminated its tediousness, purged it of its barbarous and sickening immorality, wiped it clean of cruelty and unnaturalness, selected its essentials of comedy and romance, and set them clear and sharp against a light that western eyes can bear and in an atmosphere that western lungs can breathe. Of course the new translations are interesting—especially to ethnologists and the critic with a theory that translated verse is inevitably abominable. But they are not for the general nor the artist. They include too many pages revolting by reason of unutterable brutality of incident and point of view—as also for the vileness of those lewd and dreadful puritans whose excesses against humanity and whose devotion to Islam they record—to be acceptable as literature or tolerable as reading. Now, in Galland I get the best of them. He gave me whatever is worth remembering of Bedreddin and Camaralzaman and that enchanting Fairy Peri-Banou; he is the true poet alike of Abou Hassan and the Young King of the Black Islands, of Ali Baba and the Barber of the Brothers; to him I owe that memory—of Zobeidè alone in the accursed city whose monstrous silence is broken by the voice of the one man spared by the wrath of God as he repeats his solitary prayer—which ranks with Crusoe's discovery of the footprint in the thrilling moments of my life; it was he who, by refraining from the use of pepper in his cream tarts, contrived to kitchen those confections with the very essence of romance; it was he that clove asunder the Sultan's kitchen-wall for me, and took me to the pan, and bade me ask a certain question of the fish that fried therein, and made them answer me in terms mysterious and tremendous yet. Nay, that animating and delectable feeling I cherish ever for such enchanted commodities as gold-dust and sandal-wood and sesame and cloth of gold and black slaves with scimitars—to whom do I owe it but this rare and delightful artist? 'O mes chers *Mille et une Nuits*!' says Fantasio, and he speaks in the name of all them that have lived the life that Galland alone made possible. The damsels of the new style may 'laugh till they fall backwards,' etc., through forty volumes instead of ten, and I shall still go back to my Galland. I shall go back to him because his masterpiece is—not a book of reference, nor a curiosity of literature, nor an achievement in pedantry, nor even a demonstration of the absolute failure of Islamism as an influence that makes for righteousness, but—an excellent piece of art.

RICHARDSON

His Fortune.

It is many years since Richardson fell into desuetude; it is many years since he became the novelist not of the world at large but of that inconsiderable section of the world which is interested in literature. His methods are those of a bygone epoch; his ideals, with one or two exceptions, are old-fashioned enough to seem fantastic; his sentiment belongs to ancient history; to a generation bred upon Ouida's romances and the plays of Mr. W. S. Gilbert his morality appears not merely questionable but coarse and improper and repulsive. While he lived he was adored: he moved and spoke and dwelt in an eternal mist of 'good, thick, strong, stupefying incense smoke'; he was the idol of female England, a master of virtue, a king of art, the wisest and best of mankind. Johnson revered him—Johnson and Colley Gibber; Diderot ranked him with Moses and Homer; to Balzac and Musset and George Sand he was the greatest novelist of all time; Rousseau imitated him; Macaulay wrote and talked of him with an enthusiasm that would have sat becomingly on Lady Bradshaigh herself. But all that is over. Not even the emasculation to which the late Mr. Dallas was pleased to subject his *Clarissa* could make that *Clarissa* at all popular; not all the allusions of all the leader-writers of a leader-writing age have been able to persuade the public to renew its interest in the works and ways of Grandison the august and the lovely and high-souled Harriet Byron. Richardson has to be not skimmed but studied; not sucked like an orange, nor swallowed like a lollipop, but attacked *secundum artem* like a dinner of many courses and wines. Once inside the vast and solid labyrinth of his intrigue, you must hold fast to the clue which you have caught up on entering, or the adventure proves impossible, and you emerge from his precincts defeated and disgraced. And by us children of Mudie, to whom a novel must be either a solemn brandy-and-soda or as it were a garrulous and vapid afternoon tea, adventures of that moment are not often attempted.

Pamela.

Again, when all is said in Richardson's favour it has to be admitted against him that in *Pamela* he produced an essay in vulgarity—of sentiment and morality alike—which has never been surpassed. In these days it is hardly less difficult to understand the popularity of this masterpiece of specious immodesty than to speak or think of it with patience. That it was once thought moral is as wonderful as that it was once found readable. What is more easily apprehended is the contempt of Henry Fielding—is the justice of that ridicule he was moved to visit it withal. To him, a scholar and a gentleman and a man of the world, *Pamela* was a new-fangled blend of sentimental priggishness and prurient unreality. To him the pretensions to virtue and consideration of the vulgar little hussy whom Richardson selected for his heroine were certainly not less preposterous than the titles to life and actuality of the wooden libertine whom Richardson put forth as his hero. He was artist enough to know that the book was ignoble as literature and absolutely false as fact; he was moralist enough to see that its teachings were the reverse of elevating and improving; and he uttered his conclusions *more suo* in one of the best and healthiest books in English literature. This, indeed, is the only merit of which the history of Miss Andrews can well be accused: that it set Fielding thinking and provoked him to the composition of the first of his three great novels. Pamela is only remembered nowadays as Joseph's sister: the egregious Mr. B--- has hardly any existence save as Lady Booby's brother. 'Tis an ill wind that blows good to nobody. There are few more tedious or more unpleasant experiences than *Pamela; or, Virtue Rewarded*. But you have but to remember that without it the race might never have heard of Fanny and Joseph, of the fair Slipslop and the ingenuous Didapper, of Parson Trulliber and immortal Abraham Adams, to be reconciled to its existence and the fact of its old-world fame. Nay, more, to remember its ingenious author with something of gratitude and esteem.

Grandison.

Nor is this the only charge that can be made and sustained against our poet. It is also to be noted in his disparagement that he is the author of *Sir Charles Grandison*, and that *Sir Charles Grandison*, epic of the polite virtues, is deadly dull. 'My dear,' says somebody in one of Mr. Thackeray's books, 'your eternal blue velvet quite tires me.' That is the worst of *Sir Charles Grandison*: his eternal blue velvet—his virtue, that is, his honour, his propriety, his good fortune, his absurd command over the affections of the other sex, his swordsmanship, his manliness, his patriotic sentiment, his noble piety—quite tires you. He is an ideal, but so very, very tame that it is hard to justify his existence. He is too perfect to be of the slightest moral use to anybody. He has everything he wants, so that he has no temptation to be wicked; he is incapable of immorality, so that he is easily quit of all inducements to be vicious; he has no passions, so that he is superior to every sort of spiritual contest; he is monstrous clever, so that he has made up his mind about everything knowable and unknowable; he is excessively virtuous so that he has made it up in the right direction. He is, as Mr. Leslie Stephen remarks, a tedious commentary on the truth of Mrs. Rawdon Crawley's acute reflection upon the moral effect of five thousand a year. He is only a pattern creature, because he has neither need nor opportunity, neither longing nor capacity, to be anything else. In real life such faultless monsters are impossible: one does not like to think what would happen if they were not. In fiction they are possible enough, and—what is more to the purpose—they are of necessity extravagantly dull. This is what is the matter with Sir Charles. He is dull, and he effuses dulness. By dint of being uninteresting himself he makes his surroundings uninteresting. In the record of his adventures and experiences there is enough of wit and character and invention to make the fortune of a score or more of such novels as the public of these degenerate days would hail with enthusiasm. But his function is to vitiate them all. He is a bore of the first magnitude, and of his eminence in that capacity his history is at once the monument and the proof.

Clarissa.

But if *Grandison* be dull and *Pamela* contemptible *Clarissa* remains; and *Clarissa* is what Musset called it, 'le premier roman du monde.' Of course *Clarissa* has its faults. Miss Harlowe, for instance, is not always herself—is not always the complete creation she affects to be: there are touches of moral pedantry—anticipations of George

Eliot—in her; the scenes in which she is brought to shame are scarcely real, living, moving, all the rest of it. But on the other hand is there anything better than Lovelace in the whole range of fiction? Take Lovelace in all or any of his moods—suppliant, intriguing, repentant, triumphant, above all triumphant—and find his parallel if you can. Where, you ask, did the little printer of Salisbury Court—who suggests to Mr. Stephen 'a plump white mouse in a wig'—where did Richardson discover so much gallantry and humanity, so much romance and so much fact, such an abundance of the heroic qualities and the baser veracities of mortal nature? Lovelace is, if you except Don Quixote, the completest hero in fiction. He has wit, humour, grace, brilliance, charm; he is a scoundrel and a ruffian, and he is a gentleman and a man; of his kind and in his degree he has the right Shakespearean quality. Almost as perfect in her way is the enchanting Miss Howe—an incarnation of womanliness and wit and fun, after Lovelace the most brilliant of Richardson's creations. Or take the Harlowe family: the severe and stupid father, the angry and selfish uncles, the cub James, the vixen Arabella, a very fiend of envy and hatred and malice—what a gallery of portraits is here! And Solmes and Tomlinson, Belford and Brand and Hickman; and the infinite complexity of the intrigue; the wit, the pathos, the invention; the knowledge of human nature; the faculty of dialogue—where save in *Clarissa* shall we find all these? As for Miss Harlowe herself, all incomplete as she is she remains the Eve of fiction, the prototype of the modern heroine, the common mother of all the self-contained, self-suffering, self-satisfied young persons whose delicacies and repugnances, whose independence of mind and body, whose airs and ideas and imaginings, are the stuff of the modern novel. With her begins a new ideal of womanhood; from her proceeds a type unknown in fact and fiction until she came. When after outrage she declines to marry her destroyer, and prefers death to the condonation of her dishonour, she strikes a note and assumes a position till then not merely unrecognised but absolutely undiscovered. It has been said of her half in jest and half in earnest that she is 'the aboriginal Woman's Rights person'; and it is a fact that she and Helena and Desdemona and Ophelia are practically a thousand years apart. And this is perhaps her finest virtue as it is certainly her greatest charm: that, until she set the example, woman in literature as a self-suffering individuality, as an existence endowed with equal rights to independence—of choice, volition, action—with man, had not begun to be. That of itself would suffice to make *Clarissa* memorable; and that is the least of its merits. Consider it from which point you will, the book remains a masterpiece, unique of its kind. It has been imitated but it has never been equalled. It is Richardson's only title to fame; but it is enough. Not the Great Pyramid itself is more solidly built nor more incapable of ruin.

TOLSTOÏ

The Man and the Artist.

There are two men in Tolstoï. He is a mystic and he is also a realist. He is addicted to the practice of a pietism that for all its sincerity is nothing if not vague and sentimental; and he is the most acute and dispassionate of observers, the most profound and earnest student of character and emotion. These antitheses are both represented in his novels. He has thought out the scheme of things for himself; his interpretation, while deeply tinctured with religion, is also largely and liberally human; he is one to the just and the unjust alike, and he is no more angry with the wicked than he is partial to the good. He asks but one thing of his men and women—that they shall be natural; yet he handles his humbugs and impostors with as cold a kindness and a magnanimity as equable as he displays in his treatment of their opposites. Indeed his interest in humanity is inexhaustible, and his understanding of it is well nigh formidable in its union of breadth with delicacy. Himself an aristocrat and an official, he is able to sympathise with the Russian peasant as completely and to express his sentiments as perfectly as he is able to present the characters and give utterance to the ambitions and the idiosyncrasies of the class to which he belongs and might be assumed to have studied best. It is to be noted, moreover, that he looks for his material at one or other pole of society. He is equally at home with officers and privates, with diplomats and carpenters, with princes and ploughmen; but with the intermediary strata he is out of touch, and he is careful to leave the task of presenting them to others. It is arguable that only in the highest and lowest expressions of society is unsophisticated nature to be found; and that Tolstoï, interested less in manners than in men and studious above all of the elemental qualities of character, has done right to avoid the middle-class and attach himself to the consideration and the representation of the highest and the lowest. Certain it is that here have been his successes. The Prince Andrew of *War and Peace*—cultured, intelligent, earnest, true lover and true gentleman—is as noble a hero as modern fiction has achieved; but he is no more interesting as a human being and no more successful as art than the Marianna of *les Cosaques*, who is a savage pure and simple, or the Efim of *les Deux Vieillards*, who would seem to the haughty Radical no better than a common idiot. It is to be noted of all three—the prince, the savage, and the peasant—that none in himself is sophisticate nor vile but that each is rich in the common, simple, elemental qualities of humanity. It is to these and the manifestations of these that Tolstoï turns for inspiration first of all. If he chose he could be as keen a satirist and as indefatigable a student of the meannesses and the minor miseries of existence, the toothaches and the pimples of experience, as Thackeray. But he does not choose. The epic note sounds in his work. The eternal issues of life, the fundamental interests of character and conduct and emotion, are his material. Love, valour, self-sacrifice, charity, the responsibilities of being, these and their like are the only vital facts to him; they constitute the really important part of the scheme of things as he sees and comprehends it. In their analysis the artist and the mystic meet and take hands; sometimes to each other's profit, more often, to each other's hurt. It is not without significance that no other novelist has looked so closely and penetrated so far into the secret of death: that none has divined so much of it, nor presented his results with so complete and intimate a mastery and so persuasive and inspiring a belief. Plainly Tolstoï has learned 'la vraie signification de la vie'; his faith in its capacities is immense, his acceptance of its consequences is unhesitating. He is the great optimist, and his work is wholesome and encouraging in direct ratio to the vastness of his talent and the perfection of his method.

Ivan Iliitch.

Who does not know that extraordinary *Death of Ivan Iliitch*? It is an achievement in realism: not the realism of externals and trivial details—though of this there is enough for art if not for the common Zolaphyte—but the higher and better sort, the realism which deals with mental and spiritual conditions, the realism of *Othello* and *Hamlet*. There are many deaths in literature, but there is none, I think, in which the gradual processes of dissolution are analysed and presented with such knowledge, such force, such terrible directness, as here. The result is appalling, but the final impression is one of encouragement and consolation. Here, as everywhere, Tolstoï appeals to the primitive nature of man, and the issue is what he wishes it to be. Not for him is the barren pessimism of the latter-day French rhapsodist in fiction, and the last word of his study, inexorable till then, is a word of hope and faith.

War and Peace.

Incomparably his greatest book, however, is *War and Peace*. It is the true Russian epic; alike in the vastness of its scope and in the completeness of its execution. It tells the story of the great conflict between Koutouzoff and Russia and Napoleon and France, it begins some years before Austerlitz, and it ends when Borodino and Moscow are already ancient history. The canvas is immense: the crowd of figures and the world of incidents almost bewildering. It is not a complete success. In many places the mystic has got the better of the artist: he is responsible for theories of the art of war which, advanced with the greatest confidence, are disproved by the simple narrative of events; and he has made a study of Napoleon in which, for the first and only time in all his work, he appears as an intemperate advocate. But when all is said in blame so much remains to praise that one scarce knows where to begin. Tolstoï's theory of war is mystical and untenable, no doubt; but his pictures of warfare are incomparably good. None has felt and reproduced as he has done what may be called the intimacy of battle—the feeling of the individual soldier, the passion and excitement, the terror and the fury, that taken collectively make up the influence which represents the advance or the retreat of an army in combat. But also, in a far greater degree, none has dealt so wonderfully with the vaster incidents, the more tremendous issues. His Austerlitz is magnificent; his Borodino is (there is no other word for it) epic; his studies of the Retreat are almost worthy of what has gone before. For the first time what has been called 'the peering modern touch' is here applied to great events, with the result that here is a book unique in literature. Of the characters—Natasha, Peter, Mary, Dennissoff, the Rostoffs, Helen, Dologhoff, Bagration, Bolkonsky, and the others; above all, Koutouzoff and Prince Andrew—Prince Andrew the heroic gentleman, Koutouzoff the genius of Russia and the war—to meet them once is to take on a set of friends and enemies for life.

FIELDING

Illusions.

Fielding is one of the most striking figures in our literary history, and he is one of the most popular as well. But it is questionable if many people know very much about him after all, or if the Fielding of legend—the potwalloper of genius at whom we have smiled so often—has many things in common with the Fielding of fact, the indefatigable student, the vigorous magistrate, the great and serious artist. You hear but little of him from himself; for with that mixture of intellectual egoism and moral unselfishness which is a characteristic of his large and liberal nature he was as careless of Henry Fielding's sayings and doings and as indifferent to the fact of Henry Fielding's life and personality as he was garrulous in respect of the good qualities of Henry Fielding's friends and truculently talkative about the vices of Henry Fielding's enemies. And what is exactly known people have somehow or other contrived to misapprehend and misapply. They have preferred the evidence of Horace Walpole to that of their own senses. They have suffered the brilliant antitheses of Lady Mary to obscure and blur the man as they might have found him in his work. Booth and Jones have been taken for definite and complete reflections of the author of their being: the parts for the whole, that is—a light-minded captain of foot and a hot-headed and soft-hearted young man about town for adequate presentments of the artist of a new departure and the writer of three or four books of singular solidity and finish. Whichever way you turn, you are confronted with appearances each more distorted and more dubious than the other. Some have chosen to believe the foolish fancies of Murphy, and have pictured themselves a Fielding begrimed with snuff, heady with champagne, and smoking so ferociously that out of the wrappings of his tobacco he could keep himself in paper for the manuscripts of his plays. For others the rancour of Smollett calls up a Fielding who divides his time and energy between blowing a trumpet on a Smithfield show and playing Captain Bilkum to a flesh-and-blood Stormandra at the establishment of a living, breathing, working Mother Punchbowl. With Dr. Rimbault and Professor Henry Morley others yet evolve from their inner consciousness a Fielding with a booth in Smithfield, buffooning for the coppers of a Bartlemy Fair audience. The accomplished lawyer has had as little place in men's thoughts as the tender father, the admirable artist as little as the devoted husband and the steadfast friend. Fielding has been so often painted a hard drinker that few have thought of him as a hard reader; he has been suspected of conjugal infidelity, so it has seemed impossible that he should be other than a violent Bohemian. In certain chapters

Views and Reviews

of *Jonathan Wild the Great* there is enough of sustained intellectual effort to furnish forth a hundred modern novels; but you only think of Fielding reeling home from the Rose, and refuse to consider him except as sitting down with his head in a wet towel to scribble immodest and ruffianly trash for the players! A consequence of all these exercises in sentiment and imagination has been that, while many have been ready to deal with Fielding as the text for a sermon or the subject of an essay, as the point of a moral or the adornment of a tale, few have cared to think of him as worthy to dispute the palm with Cervantes and Sir Walter as the heroic man of letters.

Facts.

He is before all things else a writer to be studied. He wrote for the world at large and to the end that he might be read eternally. His matter, his manner, the terms of his philosophy, the quality of his ideals, the nature of his achievement, proclaim him universal. Like Scott, like Cervantes, like Shakespeare, he claims not merely our acquaintance but an intimate and abiding familiarity. He has no special public, and to be only on nodding terms with him is to be practically dead to his attraction and unworthy his society. He worked not for the boys and girls of an age but for the men and women of all time; and both as artist and as thinker he commands unending attention and lifelong friendship. He is a great inventor, an unrivalled craftsman, a perfect master of his material. His achievement is the result of a life-time of varied experience, of searching and sustained observation, of unwearying intellectual endeavour. The sound and lusty types he created have an intellectual flavour peculiar to themselves. His novels teem with ripe wisdom and generous conclusions and beneficent examples. As Mr. Stephen tells you, 'he has the undeniable merit of representing certain aspects of contemporary society with a force and accuracy not even rivalled by any other writer'; and it is a fact that not to have studied him 'is to be without a knowledge of the most important documents of contemporary history.' More: to contrast those fair, large parchments in which he has stated his results with those tattered and filthy papers which the latter-day literary ragpicker exists but to grope out from kennel and sewer is to know the difference between the artist in health and the artist possessed by an idiosyncrasy as by a devil.

The Worst of It.

But the present is an age of sentiment: its ideals and ambitions are mainly emotional; what it chiefly loves is romance or the affectation of romance, passion, self-conscious solemnity, and a certain straining after picturesque effects. In Fielding's time there was doubtless a good deal of sentimentalism, for his generation delighted not only in Western and Trunnion and Mrs. Slipslop but in Pamela and Clarissa and the pathetic Le Fevre. But for all that it was—at all events in so far as it was interesting to Fielding and in so far as Fielding has pictured it—a generation that knew nothing of romance but was keenly interested in common sense, and took a vast deal of honest pleasure in humour and wit and a rather truculent and full-blooded type of satire. It is plain that such possibilities of sympathy and understanding as exist between a past of this sort and such a present as our own must of necessity be few and small. Their importance, too, is greatly diminished when you reflect on the nature and tendency of certain essential elements in Fielding's art and mind. The most vigorous and the most individual of these is probably his irony; the next is that abundant vein of purely intellectual comedy by whose presence his work is exalted to a place not greatly inferior to that of the *Misantrope* and the *Ecole des Femmes*. These rare and shining qualities are distinguishing features in the best and soundest part of Fielding. Of irony he is probably the greatest English master; of pure comedy—the intellectual manipulation and transmutation into art of what is spiritually ridiculous in manners and society—he is both in narrative and in dialogue the greatest between Shakespeare and Mr. George Meredith. And with both our sympathy is imperfect. We have learned to be sentimental and self-sufficient with Rousseau, to be romantic and chivalrous with Scott, to be emotional with Dickens, to take ourselves seriously with Balzac and George Eliot; there are touches of feeling in our laughter, even though the feeling be but spite; we have acquired a habit of politeness—a tradition of universal consideration and respect; and our theory of satire is rounded by the pleasing generalities of Mr. Du Maurier on the one hand and the malevolent respectability of Mr. W. S. Gilbert on the other. It is an age of easy writing and still easier reading: our authors produce for us much in the manner of the silkworm—only their term of life is longer; we accept their results in something of the spirit of them that are interested, and not commercially, in the processes of silkworms. And M. Guy de Maupassant can write but hath a devil, and we take him not because of his writing but because of his devil; and Blank and Dash and So-and-So and the rest could no more than so many sheep develop a single symptom of possession among them, and we take them because a devil and they are incompatibles. And art is short and time is long; and we care nothing for art and almost as much for time; and there is little if any to choose between Mudie's latest 'catch' and last year's 'sensation' at Burlington House. And to one of us it is 'poor Fielding'; and to another Fielding is merely gross, immoral, and dull; and to most the story of that last journey to Lisbon is unknown, and Thackeray's dream of Fielding—a novelist's presentment of a purely fictitious character—is the Fielding who designed and built and finished for eternity. Which is to be pitied? The artist of *Amelia* and *Jonathan Wild*, the creator of the Westerns and Parson Adams and Colonel Bath? or we the whippersnappers of sentiment—the critics who can neither read nor understand?

 the end

Views and Reviews

www.ingramcontent.com/pod-product-compliance
Lightning Source LLC
Chambersburg PA
CBHW020229170426
43201CB00007B/363